LINCOLN CHRISTIAN UNIVE

P9-CRN-216

A Syllable of Water

TWENTY WRITERS OF FAITH
REFLECT ON THEIR ART

A Syllable of Water

TWENTY WRITERS OF FAITH
REFLECT ON THEIR ART

Emilie Griffin, EDITOR

PARACLETE PRESS

BREWSTER, MASSACHUSETTS

A Syllable of Water: Twenty Writers of Faith Reflect on Their Art

2008 First printing

Copyright © 2008 by The Chrysostom Society

ISBN 978-1-55725-566-2

"The Novel Taking Form: On Building Fiction" by Doris Betts appeared, in slightly altered form, as the essay, "Whispering Hope," in *Image: a Journal of the Arts and Religion*, Issue #7, Fall 1994. Used by permission.

Library of Congress Cataloging-in-Publication Data

A syllable of water : twenty writers of faith reflect on their art / edited by Emilie Griffin.
    p. cm.
  Includes bibliographical references and index.
  ISBN 978-1-55725-566-2 (alk. paper)
  1. Christian literature—Authorship. 2. Authorship. I.Griffin, Emilie.
  BR44.S95 2008
  808'.06623—dc22   2008034267

10 9 8 7 6 5 4 3 2 1

All rights reserved. No portion of this book may be reproduced, stored in an electronic retrieval system, or transmitted in any form or by any means—electronic, mechanical, photocopy, recording, or any other—except for brief quotations in printed reviews, without the prior permission of the publisher.

Published by Paraclete Press
Brewster, Massachusetts
www.paracletepress.com

Printed in the United States of America

Contents

Introduction   vii
  The Word Made Flesh
  Robert Siegel

Part One
BEGINNINGS, DISCIPLINES, TOOLS & FAITH

1 Gushers and Bleeders: On Getting Started   3
  Harold Fickett

2 Within Infinite Purposes: On Writing and Place   11
  John Leax

3 The Writer's Notebook: On Journal Keeping   23
  Luci Shaw

4 Realms of Gold and Stout Cortez: 36
  On Why Writers Ought to Read Widely and Well
  Dain Trafton

5 Getting It Right: On Research   48
  Rudy Nelson

6 A Twitch Upon the Thread: On Writing as an   61
  Act of Faith
  Emilie Griffin

7 Entering into the Dark and Essential Places   70
  That Writing Demands: On Writer's Block
  Keith Miller

Part Two
GENRES

8 Deeper Subjects: On Writing Creative Nonfiction   83
  James Calvin Schaap

133180

9 The Novel Taking Form: On Building Fiction   94
   Doris Betts

10 Being Smarter Than We Are: On the Short Story   104
   Erin McGraw

11 Narrating Our Lives: On Memoir   116
   Virginia Stem Owens

12 Steep and Exhilarating Mountains of Playwriting: 129
   On Drama
   Jeanne Murray Walker

13 A Troubled and Troubling Mirror: On Poetry   142
   Scott Cairns

14 The Literature of Fact: On the Writer as Journalist 154
   Philip Yancey

15 Made Visible and Plain: On Spiritual Writing   168
   Richard J. Foster

16 Babylon, Babel, Babble: On Translation (Part I)   180
   William Griffin

17 Word and Spirit: On Translation (Part II)   188
   Eugene H. Peterson

Part Three
ENDINGS

18 After the Fire of Writing: On Revision   199
   Diane Glancy

19 Offstage: On the Writer and the Editor   210
   John Wilson

Contributors   221
The Chrysostom Society   227

The Word Made Flesh

Robert Siegel

*Who has heard
the moonlit stream speak
a syllable of water?*

Imagine you have the chance to spend an hour alone with a well-published writer while he shares with you secrets of his art or she reveals how her art relates to her faith. In a sense, this is the experience awaiting you with the twenty authors of this book. Collectively, they've written everything from poetry and fiction to drama and nonfiction, and here they share their experience with other writers, both new and seasoned, and with other readers. They cover a range of topics—from putting the first words down on paper to polishing the manuscript, in addition to their lives and the faith that informs their calling.

Though no book can be completely comprehensive, a glance at the table of contents reveals that this one touches on all the topics usually addressed in a creative writing course—even more than are normally covered in a semester. In addition to the usual chapters devoted to poetry, the novel, the short story, drama, and nonfiction, the book includes chapters on getting started, the writer's place, the writer's notebook, writer's block, reading, research, memoirs, journalism, spiritual writing, translation, revision, editing, and writing as an act of faith.

All the contributors to this volume are members of the Chrysostom Society, a group of writers who gather once a year to share their writing and their Christian faith. We come from a wide range of denominations, from Roman Catholic to Quaker, Baptist to Greek Orthodox, and represent every genre of writing. At our yearly gatherings, we inspire and encourage one another, talk shop, and share writerly insights; we worship and play together. The idea for this book came out of one such meeting. We conceived of it as a book that would do for others some of what we do for ourselves in our gatherings. By relating our writing experience from a personal point of view, we aim to share with new and established writers not only our differing approaches to our art, but also our art's integral relation to our faith.

In doing so, we hope to give helpful tips to the new writer, but also to go beyond questions of craft and aesthetics. We believe that good writing has a value beyond its own excellence and the talent of the author. It is ultimately about something—the substance of this world and what lies beyond the world. As J.R.R. Tolkien believed, we are subcreators, responding to the One who made us in the same mode by which we're made. To that end, we have labored to ensure that this is not simply another book on how to write, but a sharing of personal insights into the writer's life and craft, especially as they relate to his or her deepest convictions.

The chapters may be read in any order that's convenient to your needs or wishes. Teachers using it may wish to assign chapters in the order subjects are taken up in class. We hope that each chapter might be a bit like having the author in class for a day, where he or she would share intimately and honestly what it is like to answer the vocation of writing within the larger context of life and faith.

We writers are notoriously independent creatures. But one aim most of us share is a desire to call up things into words. This is the alchemy that fascinates us. A sensation, impression, or image will step out from its surroundings and demand our total attention. The thing itself will appear to rise up as words and send us fumbling for our notebooks. Here is the wonder of what Keats called "natural magic"—as the image reaches up toward the words, the words become the image, the thing itself. For one happy moment, they are fused. Thing becomes word and word becomes thing in a process far deeper in the workings of the universe than we know. Substance and meaning are fused. The terrible gap between experience and the articulation of experience is closed. The mind is one with what it perceives.

The title of this book, *A Syllable of Water,* taken from the poem above,* may serve as an example of this fusion of word and thing. The sound of the moonlit stream seems to utter "a syllable" to the speaker: water and word become one. They fuse, aided by the liquid sound of *syllable.* This fusion offers to both reader and writer what some have called a "unitive experience." The fusion of observer and observed in aesthetic experience is a form of union. Our best experiences with literature and the arts are contemplative, a union of ourselves with the beauty before us. Literature and the arts can help us to forget ourselves and experience a completeness, a wholeness, for a moment or an hour. We forget our incomplete, divided selves, and for a time are made one with what we are contemplating. This unitive experience can lead us to see beyond the work of art itself to what may shine through it, the world of the spirit.

This fusion also reminds us that good writing must appeal to the senses—to the body as well as to our emotions and our minds. By appealing to our senses, good writing incarnates our meaning. This is perhaps the first lesson a writer must learn—and one we continue to learn all our lives. After all, it is through our senses more than through our thoughts that we remember certain moments in literature. Long after reading it, we recall poet Gerard Manley Hopkins's celebration in "Pied Beauty" of "rose moles all in stipple upon trout that swim," a perfect detail easily overlooked by fishermen who may have caught a thousand trout. Nor are we likely to forget the images in Wallace

Stevens's lament that "Children picking up our bones / Will never know that these were once / As quick as foxes on the hill." Similarly, who can forget Pablo Neruda, in his "Ode to the Tomato," describing a ripe one cut in half as "a fresh, / deep, / inexhaustible / sun"?

Writing that appeals to the senses is more than vivid and memorable. For those of us who are Christians, it is incarnational. As in Christ the Word became flesh, so we hope our own best words become flesh. We trust they will incarnate the beauty, terror, and glory of this world even as they lift the reader's gaze in hope beyond it. For we believe the incarnate Word, or Logos, of God is the transcendent element in every word.

Above all we wish to honor the One who might say (as I imagine him),

> *I am all these, and yet none:*
> *Not the red streams flooding the banks of cells*
> *nor the river hungry for the ocean*
> *nor the crow's feather that dandles to the ground*
> *nor the wind trafficking in perfume*
> *nor the little pool holding a syllable of water.*
>
> *Still, I am where the tongue presses the roof of the mouth,*
> *in the crease of the closed hand,*
> *in the foot hesitating on the stoop,*
> *in the eye that draws its shape on the sky*
> *and lingers, waiting for the face of light.*

Robert Siegel
President, The Chrysostom Society, 2004–2007

---

*"Who has Heard" and the lines from "Neti, Neti" closing this introduction are the author's, the latter from *A Pentecost of Finches: New and Selected Poems* (Paraclete Press, 2006).

Part One

BEGINNINGS, DISCIPLINES, TOOLS & FAITH

1

Gushers and Bleeders
On Getting Started

Harold Fickett

Getting started puts most writers in a sweat. The blank page holds unlimited possibilities, but the first sentence eliminates too many options, as it establishes the writer's voice and indicates the text's scope. Apart from these paralyzing considerations is the humble matter of how, when, and where to begin. Does one need a room of one's own? Is there some magic in a Mont Blanc pen? Or gigahertz and gigabytes? And how, in a world that demands so much, can you find the time and the pluck to address the universe? This last question bears down on writers who work in longer forms, such as the novel, where the endless task of writing can seem like "crawling on one's knees from Moscow to Vladivostok."

Most of these questions resolve themselves, if we let them, in the same way that difficulties resolve themselves when we begin physical or spiritual exercise. Much of life is about showing up. We may not feel like going to the gym or hitting our knees, but once there we are almost certain to start working out or praying. The best advice for how to get started was given by Flannery O'Connor to one of her correspondents: Sit at your desk for three hours each morning. Don't allow yourself to read, answer phone calls, tidy up, or anything else. You sit there. If you are not writing, you still sit there. Eventually, you *will* write.

Of course, few have the luxury of free mornings. (As to this, O'Connor recommended a life without encumbrances, or finding a wealthy spouse.) But, as a writer, you need to do what you can, as you can, and devote clear-headed hours to the task.

One prize-winning writer, reflecting on how her career began, recalled her writing schedule while her children were growing up. She had only one hour each day, from ten to eleven in the morning, but she religiously devoted that hour to writing. She commented that she was almost as productive during that period of her life as she was later when her time was entirely free. I have a friend, Davis Bunn, who launched his own career as a novelist by devoting the first two hours of every day to the task, even as he flew around Europe as the director of an international business advisory group.

As with everything else in writing, the three-hours-in-the-morning advice is always true except when it isn't. There are advocates of marathon sessions, such as the late John Gardner, who boasted of his fifteen-hour workdays and warned young writers they had better do likewise. Victor Hugo remains the most successful practitioner of around-the-clock writing. He'd pile up debts until he was about to be thrown in the poorhouse and then stoke himself with stimulants and absinthe until he finished long novels in record time. James Baldwin liked to work through the night; he'd begin by taking a sip of a drink, and then work away while the ice cubes melted and night eventually turned to day. Vladimir Nabokov, a writer of wonderful density, actually began by writing sentences on three-by-five cards and carrying these around in his jacket, shirt, and pants pockets until he could lay out a book in rough form.

To writers who are anxious about how to begin, I always recommend reading *The Paris Review Interviews*. These long discussions with such figures as William Faulkner, Toni Morrison, Isaac Bashevis Singer, Graham Greene, James Baldwin, Stephen King, Philip Larkin, Eudora Welty, Peter Carey, and Gabriel García Márquez will disabuse anyone of the notion that there's one right way to proceed. (Or even a right way to conceive of their own work: Gabriel García Márquez, the father of magical realism, confesses that he strives to present the truth in as *journalistic* a way as possible—not what anyone would have imagined about the conjurer of flowers raining at the death of Remedios the Beauty.)

What I can say with some measure of assurance is that writers who keep at it discover the ways they work best and then often display unparalleled energy and discipline in these habits.

But for beginning writers, the only way to begin to address the worries and other human frailties that plague all writers is to preserve as many clear-headed hours as you can for writing, and then write. As you begin, you'll probably fall into one of two camps of first-time composition: you'll be either a gusher or a bleeder, and this will partly determine the type of habits you need to cultivate. Gushers are like Thomas Wolfe, whose famous editor, Maxwell Perkins, compared his lyrical prose in *Look Homeward Angel* to a Mississippi River without banks. Writing poured out of Wolfe in super-abundance, but he had so little feel for structure that Perkins served as a one-man Corps of Engineers. The great spiritual writer of the twentieth century, Thomas Merton, was also a gusher, a trait that allowed him to produce an astounding volume of work between prayer offices as a Trappist monk.

Gushers generally have a hard time learning to edit their work or even valuing the editing of others, as they tend to mistake further elaboration for editing. If you are a gusher, let it flow when it flows, but then be prepared for a reckoning. Disabuse yourself of the notion that mania equates with greatness. How the writer feels during composition rarely says much about the work's value. Gushers have to face the paradoxical truth that good work can get done—and often demands to be done—in the midst of the humdrum days, even during times of depression.

Bleeders are painfully slow at composition and often prefer rewriting to original composition. In my own case, composition is rather like trying to force kielbasa through cheesecloth—it's a constipated procedure. I love it when there's something already on the page. As Annie Dillard remarked, I like to make a mess and then clean it up. I much prefer a mess to a blank slate, as do most bleeders, although there are some exacting types among bleeders, such as my old teacher, the late novelist John Hawkes, who wrote very slowly but then revised little. He would get a paragraph sounding just right before proceeding to the next, and he usually wrote a page or less per day.

Bleeders often have a hard time keeping their internal editor from interfering with—if not bringing to a dead halt—invention. Every writer needs to be two writers: an inventor and an editor. Bleeders like me do well to turn off their critical apparatus when composing and let their delight in the language and the unexpected take over. When writing fiction or poetry, they need to watch the "vivid and continuous dream" in their mind's eye, as John Gardner described it. Transport is all-important in writing, and the reader will not experience it if the writer doesn't first. As Madeleine L'Engle used to say, "When I write, I write; I don't think."

Bleeders can also be hyperanxious that the imaginary sense of being lifted out of one's circumstances will never arrive onto the page. On the other hand, discipline comes more naturally to bleeders, and they usually keep their appointments with inspiration. It's helpful to assume the confident attitude of one writer who said: "I sit down at 8:00 AM. At 8:01 I am inspired."

Whether you are a gusher or a bleeder, feel free to make a mess; you'll be rewarded by the chance to clean it up.

Becoming a Star?

Besides the mechanical impediments to getting started, there are deeper psychological and spiritual traps to be negotiated. Beginning brings with it anxiety. Any time you commit words to the page, you are placing yourself and how you will be regarded on the line.

Today, as I write this, the room is empty and quiet, with nothing beyond my computer screen but a thermostat and vent on a white wall. And yet here I am, nervous as a cat, obsessively scratching my bald spot. I'm feeling a similar anxiety to what I would experience speaking before a packed house. Among the crowd sit the ghosts of my old teachers and high school classmates to whom I bragged of what I would one day become. I'm before *you,* hoping to dazzle, to persuade, to provide a service, to win approval and whatever prizes go with it. Writing is the act of a closeted performer. It drives straight to the deepest of human motivations: to be known and to be loved.

There was an old *New Yorker* cartoon showing a writer at his typewriter on a summer cottage porch with his wife whispering into his ear, "Johnny Carson, Dick Cavett, Merv Griffin." Today, the names would include Leno and Letterman and, certainly, Oprah. Freud said that writers were after sex and money, and he was right. But then, sex and money are loci of many other human meanings—to be received, to be validated, to have your life count or to be redeemed from all that hasn't counted.

The stakes are high, so we feel at risk of negative judgments—that we are not worthy, that our offerings are unacceptable, that no one wants to know us or love us. Of course, our existence as humans does not consist in words on a page—thank God. Truly, thank God. But the words on the page are so personal that the reality of this distinction can be hard to maintain.

Indeed, literary culture presumes that nothing counts but the work. "Real writers" can be alcoholics, fail multiple times at marriage, neglect their children, and make concubines of their graduate assistants, and these behaviors can be seen as merely the frissons of their real life—the part that made a lasting contribution to literature or at least garnered the lead review in *The New York Times* Sunday supplement.

Jean-Paul Sartre said that people found their status as *beings* intolerable, as it confronted them with constant choices and shifting

judgments. That's why we aspire to the status of a known quantity—
in fact, a divine being. Everyone's fundamental project, according to
Sartre, is to be God. So, insurance salesmen hang plaques on the wall
declaring they are "Million-Dollar Sellers." In the same way, writers
want to be literary stars—they want their silk-screened picture hung
in Barnes & Noble alongside Toni Morrison and Michael Chabon.
They want to be a "real writer," no longer subject to the slings and
arrows of fortune; or to what we most fear: inadequacy, anonymity,
failure, neglect, abuse.

I remember going into City Lights Bookstore in San Francisco and
seeing framed photographs of my early literary heroes, Gary Snyder,
Jack Kerouac, Henry Miller, and Allen Ginsberg, who were intimately
connected with this place that became a cultural icon of the fifties and
sixties. The owner of City Lights, Lawrence Ferlinghetti, was also an
inspiration to me as a teenager. I loved his *A Coney Island of the Mind,*
which was probably the first poetry I read outside a literature class,
and a book that taught me about language as a living phenomenon.
Being in the store reminded me of how much I loved the work of
Ferlinghetti and his friends as a young man, and how I thought that
joining their company would translate to becoming divine in some
way. But the store's cultivated shabbiness reminded me that those
dreams of divinity were just another form of celebrity worship, with
its unreal character and expectations. (The beats and the hippies never
got over equating dirt and disarray with freedom.) While Hollywood
has nearly perfected celebrity as a reasonable facsimile of the divine,
literary culture doesn't quite know how to spangle the heavens.

These reflections brought me down from the imaginary heights to
what I know now, from long practice, writing can be: a fascinating
job and a valuable service. The job involves performing and learning,
and the hard labor of combining the two. As writers, we teach and
entertain. We also explore the mystery of being human and provide
symbolic expressions of *beauty,* which is the glory of God shining

in creation. The anxiety that goes with being a performer and venturing into the unknown is inescapable—an inevitable burden of the occupation. Philosopher Søren Kierkegaard said that man must choose between anxiety and boredom, and choosing to write certainly decides that question.

We write in order to provide a service for others, to teach and to delight, to speak as best we can of what cannot be expressed otherwise, and in turn earn a living or garner other legitimate rewards. The act of writing is really not any more exalted than that, except in the following regard: writing, when undertaken rightly, can assist in our own redemption. The same is true of all vocations, but it's worthwhile to note writing's particular affinities with the Christian life.

Making up stories and commiting them to the page is fun, and I would even venture to say that it makes God happy. Writing allows us to participate in a process that's analogous to God's own creation, awakening us to what lies beyond ourselves. Every invention—of an essay, a poem, a novel, even a recipe—is an instance of ecstasy. Ideas, particularly original ideas, take us out of ourselves and into another world. They spring forth in seeming perfection, like Athena from the head of Zeus. Then, in fleshing out the world of an idea, we use words that derive from the creative reason of the world, the Logos, the Christ through whom all things were made. We were given this privilege when we were made in the image of God, and gratitude for this gift can draw us closer to God.

But imaginative creation is a world away from *being God,* which is creativity's idol. Rather, the act of writing invites us both to know our frailty—and the anxiety that comes with it—and to experience God's image being continually transformed into a sharper likeness. If we begin with such an end in view, our work will be an offering and not an idol, and getting started will be an appointment worth keeping for all its anxieties.

FURTHER READING

The starting writer should stock his or her library with at least two style manuals, the perennially helpful *The Elements of Style* by Strunk and White, and the comprehensive *The Chicago Manual of Style*.

As noted in the essay, I recommend *The Paris Review Interviews* as a means of surveying the many ways writers pursue the craft. Annie Dillard's *The Writing Life* is jam-packed with helpful and wonderful anecdotes, particularly about the craziness of getting started. John Gardner's *The Art of Fiction* teaches lessons that apply across the genres. Walker Percy's *Lost in the Cosmos* includes a hilarious section on why writers drink that also speaks to the anxieties that beginning a writing project entails.

2

Within Infinite Purposes
On Writing and Place

———•———

John Leax

> If we understand this concept of place carefully and fully enough, we can say simply that to be in place is good and to be out of place is evil, for where we are with respect to our place both in the order of things and on earth is the definition of our whereabouts with respect to God and our fellow creatures.
>
> —Wendell Berry, "Poetry and Place"

Recently, a writer visiting the campus where I teach asked to see the place I write. We walked the winding path across my quarter-acre yard, past the white garden, the water gardens, the butterfly garden, through the vegetables to the small cabin I built with hand tools in the corner farthest from the house. As we approached it, he remarked, "I'm beginning to feel envy." I admit I'm proud of my writing studio. Six by eight, it is made of locally cut, rough-sawn hemlock and softened by overhanging forsythia and lilac bushes. I like the way it looks.

I like the inside even more, and my writer friend agreed. The walls are white. The ceiling is natural wood. On the wall opposite the door, six fishing rods await free moments. Above them a collection of antique bait casting and fly reels line a shelf. Nearly half the floor space is taken up by a desk placed so the light comes over my left shoulder from a large window. I have one chair, an unabridged dictionary, and a bookcase filled with boxes of manuscripts in various stages of completion.

That's it. My writing place. There is no room for anyone else. And yet, I am not alone here, for I am placed not only in my garden, but in a tradition of literary agrarians who value the health of the earth and the health of culture. I converse with writers widely separated in time—living writers such as Wendell Berry, great modernists such as Robert Frost, traditionally studied figures such as William Wordsworth and Alexander Pope, ancients such as Virgil. Knowing I speak to my time from within a long tradition empowers me. These writers give me freedom to concern myself with the particular, local community of my neighborhood and to believe that that can be sufficient.

As I sit in my studio, I often forget that I am a privileged man. I need to remember that Russian writer Alexander Solzhenitzen wrote under duress in a prison camp. Keats wrote in the anguish of ill health and poverty. As a group, women have suffered more than men. Virginia Woolf's classic *A Room of One's Own* is nothing less than an exposition of how a person without a place is silenced.

When Woolf asked, "What conditions are necessary for the creation of works of art?" she was, of course, addressing the topic of women and fiction. It would be disingenuous of me to hijack her text for my own purposes, but I am willing to risk it, for her conclusion, "a woman must have money and a room of her own," has import beyond the silencing of women. Her conclusion acknowledges the truth of what is necessary for any writer. Without a belief that one dwells in an authority-granting place, that one is empowered to speak, neither man nor woman can write.

The mythic story of power deriving from place is the story of Antaeus. A giant and irresistible wrestler, Antaeus derived his power from his connection to the earth. As long as his body remained in contact with the ground, he could not be defeated. Thrown down, he would rise up stronger. An insecure, defensive fellow, he constantly challenged strangers to wrestle, defeated them, and killed them.

Hercules, understanding the source of Antaeus's strength, lifted him from the ground and strangled him as he grew weak.

The story appears to be simple, but I find it full of ambiguities.

To start with, Antaeus is xenophobic. He lives in violation of the rule of hospitality. He is a villain for whom a connection to place is nothing more than an excuse to denigrate and abuse the stranger. How surprisingly like the university Beadle who rose up in "horror and indignation" when Virginia Woolf ventured off the gravel path onto the turf that belonged only to "the Fellows and Scholars."

The trickster Hercules isn't much better. Though many of his deeds are heroic and directed at monsters, he is finally a professional show-off, a perpetual stranger as incapable of transcending his own interests as Antaeus. And, like Antaeus, he lives by deeds of violence.

The power that comes from place, if it is to be good, must be something other than the power to assert dominance. Neither Antaeus's defensive possession of his place, nor Hercules's globalizing destruction of Antaeus's connection offers us much hope for understanding what it means to be empowered by having a place.

⌒

Born during the height of World War II, I did not know my father until I was three. On my father's return from Europe, my family returned to dwell on Leax Lane, a dirt road winding up a wooded hillside past houses occupied by family. The day we made that return was the day my brother was born. Though I know now how difficult the 1940s were for my parents, those early years of my childhood remain the Eden of my imagination. Exile came in third grade. My youngest uncle, a boy just a few years older than I was, found an "unloaded" shotgun and accidentally shot my mother. To placate my mother's family, my father agreed to move off the hill. For four years we lived in suburbia, and then we moved to the countryside. Three years later, I went away to prep school. My one constant friend, as I grew, was the landscape of western Pennsylvania.

During my college years, I ranged restlessly from one college to another, never settling into any community. Finally, at Houghton College, I met a group of faculty who took me in. I didn't satisfy them with my work—I was an intractable student, spending as much time wandering the pastoral hills and fishing the Genesee River as studying—but they seemed to understand I was seeking to find a place in the world and to understand my compulsion to write. My senior year I married, and order entered my life.

I did not become orderly, but I began to define what mattered. Preparing to be married, I rented and painted a small apartment over the only store in town. With the hand tools I kept in my room—my father had been a carpenter, and I went nowhere without a hammer, saw, square, and rule—I built end tables and bookcases. I made a place for the marriage to begin.

After graduate school, I accepted an invitation to return to Houghton and join them in the English department. I thought I'd stay a year or two and move on. Houghton, I imagined, would prove too small, too rural, too far from the literary centers I wanted to reach.

I've stayed forty years, and will likely stay a few more.

I became conscious that place mattered to me when I purchased Wendell Berry's book of essays *The Long-Legged House* at the end of my first year of teaching. Reading his prose was not so much a matter of coming under the influence of a master as it was discovering a voice that could help me know who I was and who I should become. In the title essay, Berry described the first summer of his marriage:

I began that summer of my marriage the surprisingly long and difficult labor of *seeing* the country I had been born in and had lived my life in until then. I think that this was peculiarly important and necessary to me; for whereas most American writers—even most Americans—of my time are displaced persons, I am a placed person. For longer than I can remember, both sides of my family have lived within five or six miles of this riverbank where the old Camp stood and where I sit writing now.

The words shocked and excited me. I had been mourning for and writing about the Leax family diaspora in the 1950s. One after another, my six uncles and aunts had moved to better addresses. My generation was scattering farther. I was the first to move away, and I was losing touch with my cousins. There was nothing unusual about our family's story. It was nothing more or less than the story of "the greatest generation," but it had left me out of state, an exile longing for home.

Eight years later, after a sabbatical spent asking questions about how I wanted to live, I knew I could never be a person placed as Berry is placed. By then no Leaxes remained on Leax Lane. But I also knew I could stop my own movement. I realized I had, in fact, stopped. I had come to rest in the place where my marriage had begun. Suddenly I understood I could make my being where I was intentional. I could choose to make my work as a person and as a writer the work of belonging.

⌒

When I made that choice thirty years ago, I had already lived "in place" for ten years. I had begun to think about my life in community, and I had begun to think about what it meant to my work to belong to that community. I was not naïve. But neither was I particularly informed about my choice.

Place is an elusive term. The *Oxford English Dictionary* discussion begins with the idea of a town square. It moves quickly, however, to speak of the position of a body in space in relation to other bodies, implying one can be placed only in a relationship. Wallace Stegner writes in *Where the Bluebird Sings to the Lemonade Springs* that "no place is a place until it has had a poet." I take Stegner to mean that the idea of place cannot be separated from story, for it is story that reveals the meaningful relationships in the square of human habitation and discourse. That idea, of course, instantly becomes metaphorical, and one moves to the discussion of one's place or position in a social order. What place does one deserve at the table? Is one place more appropriate for one than another? What does it mean to be out of place? Is one granted a room of one's own? What does it mean to be home?

All that I have to say about place grows from the central metaphor of my life: as a Christian, I speak of being in Christ. In my journal, *In Season and Out,* written just a few years after choosing to stay in place, I reflected: "The Christian has only one place to be. In Christ. Having that one place to be—which is no place and every place—frees the Christian from having to be going anywhere. . . . As I understand this, by choosing to stay where I am, where Christ has placed me, I act out my resting in him." I have found since writing those words that rather than simplifying anything, having one's place in Christ complicates one's life, for the range of relationships, the spiritual ecology, is all inclusive. The relationships exist in the ever-unfolding work of Christ in bringing the Creation, of which we are a part, into completion within his infinite purposes. I am in place in a process that remains beyond my comprehension.

Though I have chosen to live out this metaphor by staying in and exploring one place, other writers have focused on the presence of Christ in all places, and have worked the metaphor in relationship to the kingdom of God, a kingdom without boundaries that ranges across space and cultures. Either way, we find our voices and speak to others from our place in Christ.

⌒

The geographer Yi-Fu Tuan writes in *Topophilia:* "People everywhere tend to structure space—geographical and cosmological—with themselves at the center and with concentric zones (more or less well defined) of decreasing value beyond." We might think of this center as home. We might also think of it as the place where we are known.

For a number of years I wrote a newspaper column for our local daily newspaper. One particularly bitter February when I was following with some distress the news of the hardships being endured by the poor of Eastern Europe, I wrote a piece reflecting on the ease of our lives and our casual expectations of comfort. A few days after the column appeared, my wife and I were having dinner at a local restaurant. A man came up to our table and said, "You're the writer aren't you?" As I rose to greet him, I knew I'd been recognized. I had spoken within and to my local community and I was about to be held accountable. "I have relatives in Eastern Europe," he said. "You got it right, and I appreciate it." For the next moments of conversation, we stood together, home in the center where we answer to each other and where we stand open by our words to the needs of the whole world.

More than once I have been tempted to abandon my residency, but each time I have looked at what I have gained by being in place and I have chosen to stay. In "Poetry and Place" Wendell Berry writes, "Things in nature cohere, and humans rightly belong to that coherence, but on the peculiarly human condition that if they are to belong to it, and not destroy it (and themselves), they must consciously join it." How can one join that coherence except by investing oneself in a place where it becomes visible?

I once participated in a grassroots movement to prevent the building of a nuclear waste dump on a hillside just upstream from my house. My backyard is the place I know best. As writers, if we know a place well enough to protect it intelligently, and have enough character to honor others' backyards, writing can be the place through which, by responsible action, we enter the coherence. It can be the point where we join our interests with those of a larger community, including the earth, the plants, the animals, and the people all dwelling together.

This joining of ourselves as writers to the earth and to others within the "concentric circles of affiliation" is, I believe, crucial. I can't return to Leax Lane, but by choosing my quarter-acre near the Genesee River, I submit to the demands of the place I have come to and open myself to the influence of concerns larger than my own. In that submission I become responsible.

When I was a teenager, one of my mother's favorite phrases was, "It's not what you say; it's how you say it." I hated those words, but I understand now, in reminding me to respect my audience, she was teaching me a lesson vital to writing to and for a place, a community. One cannot long disrespect one's neighbors and continue to live in the neighborhood.

Knowing our first audience knows us as well as we know ourselves guarantees that we approach our subject with, at least, humility and, at best, love. Membership in the neighborhood grounds me as a writer. Just as Leax Lane once gave me identity and words, my place in the Genesee Valley gives me voice. Home, however, can be narrow and stultifying. Often it cannot meet the needs of the restless, intelligent, and creative. I remember attending a meeting with eighty other parents at the local K–12 regional school when my daughter entered junior high. The guidance counselor tried to talk about college preparation. One parent asked plaintively, "Why? You educate our children to go away." She, of course, was right. Our small towns, even our suburban or city neighborhoods, often seem puny and confining once we're exposed to the larger world. Sometimes to counter this feeling of inferiority or provincialism, we protest too much. Like Antaeus, we become xenophobic and scorn the outsider. We forbid Virginia Woolf to walk on the grass. Yet, Christ's parable of the Samaritan traveler warns us against such narrowness. Our neighbor is the one who needs us. There can be no limit to our concern or our generosity.

The Genesee Valley I live in is both a natural and a man-made landscape. Hillsides that were once farm fields are now second growth forest. Before they were fields, they were covered with white pine. Within my memory, a section of the river has straightened out a bend and moved from one side of the valley to the other. That migration was the result of both farming practices and the flooding following Hurricane Agnes in 1972. To comprehend my place in the created order of this environment requires me to understand science, to know the succession of trees, to understand erosion. It also requires me to understand how the values and ambitions of my culture have determined the very shape of the physical world.

To be at home in the Genesee Valley, I must also know something of the human story of this place. I must understand how the native peoples of the Five Nations used the river and inhabited the valley and hills. I must understand how their life was succeeded by farmers and by the builders of the Genesee Canal. I must understand how the railroad displaced both the canal and agrarian prosperity and encouraged westward migration. I must understand ecological and social history. These histories are the stories Wallace Stegner alludes to. Because I live within them, I am as much theirs as they are mine. Telling them is my task.

Urban neighborhoods and suburbs are places with stories to be learned and told just as surely as my rural neighborhood. My agrarian concerns for place and culture reach there as well. Wendell Berry once wrote, "We are all as dependent on the earth as the earthworm." We all eat. And we are all dependent on each other. If you are a city dweller, your task is to tell the story of your city so that I and other readers might have entry into the richness of Christ's being in all places. Story by story, we comprehend the fullness of grace.

Telling the stories of a changing, evolving place from within it requires all of us, as writers, to consider our relation to other writers, to our place in a literary tradition. On the simplest level, this requires us to learn what has been done, to master the conventions of our craft. For me, this means recognizing that I come after Pope and Wordsworth and Frost—to name a few masters I admire. My forms are built on theirs.

This, fortunately, does not mean that we are limited to repeating what these masters have done. A tradition is a living thing, and just as the Genesee River migrates back and forth across its valley and remains the same river, the actual expressions of a tradition are rich, varied, and marked by the personalities of writers.

The best discussion of the dynamic nature of tradition I know is found in T.S. Eliot's essay, "Tradition and the Individual Talent." Eliot writes:

> No poet, no artist of any art, has his complete meaning alone. His significance, his appreciation is the appreciation of his relation to the dead poets and artists. You cannot value him alone. . . . what happens when a new work of art is created is something that happens simultaneously to all the works of art which preceded it. The existing monuments form an ideal order among themselves, which is modified by the introduction of the new (the really new) work of art among them. The existing order is complete before the new work arrives; for order to persist after the supervention of novelty, the whole existing order must be, if ever so slightly, altered; and so the relations, proportions, values of each work of art toward the whole are readjusted; and this is conformity between the old and the new.

For Eliot, for any writer seeking to have a place in the tradition, "fitting in" is a significant measure of value. Virginia Woolf, in her discussion of women and fiction in the book *A Room of One's Own,* made the same observation: "For books continue each other, in spite of our habit of judging them separately." And she lamented that women of her generation had no tradition behind them to offer them a place fitting to their gifts. Isolated, they had no community to hold them accountable, no community in which to find their value.

One must have a place within the literary tradition to produce good work, and just as with one's place within the created order and within a community, that place must be both granted and chosen. Fortunately, we have come to understand the literary tradition enlarged to include Virginia Woolf, but her point remains. To be placeless is to be silenced.

⁓

Where is my writing place? The quick answer is in a tiny cabin in the corner of a garden in the Genesee Valley. But that answer misses the richness of place in my writing and my life. The cabin is a place I have made within a community that has granted me membership in the ever-shifting, ever-changing relationships of its physical and spiritual ecology. My writing place is the land community: the soils, waters, plants, creatures, neighbors, and friends, first of this valley and then of the whole world. It is also a tradition, literary and cultural. It exists in the ever-unfolding work of Christ in bringing his Creation into completion within his infinite purposes.

FURTHER READING

The body of work that could be described as a self-conscious literature of place emerged in the second half of the twentieth century. It is closely related to agrarianism and to literary environmentalism. One of the most accessible books is Scott Russell Sanders's *Staying Put,* an extended essay about making a home in the Midwest. A second book by Sanders, *Writing from the Center,* explicitly develops the connection of place and writing. The essays of the Kentucky poet Wendell Berry are essential to this movement. His early, largely narrative essays "The Long-Legged House" and "A Native Hill" are the best starting point for exploring his work. From those, one should proceed to "The Making of a Marginal Farm." These three essays are collected in *Recollected Essays: 1965–1980*. Berry addresses place more formally in two later essays, "People, Land, and Community" and "Poetry and Place," both found in *Standing by Words*. Anyone interested in a more theoretical literary criticism should consider Lawrence Buell's *Writing for an Endangered World* and J. Scott Bryson's *The West Side of Any Mountain: Place, Space, and Ecopoetry.*

3

The Writer's Notebook
On Journal Keeping

———

Luci Shaw

In the dreamy, carefree days of childhood, with freedom to wander and explore fields and forests and streams in Australia, where I grew up, the most magical time of any day for me was dusk. Moon showed her face. The Southern Cross patterned the evening sky. And the lightning bugs began to flicker their signals in the shadows under the eucalyptus trees. Stop. Go.

I'd run to the house to get my "collection jar," a mason jar with holes punched in the metal lid so that the lightning bugs (also called glowworms Down Under) could "breathe." I'd snatch a wisp of grass, or a eucalyptus leaf, and drop it in the bottom of the jar, to help my little jewel bugs feel at home, and then I'd begin my scavenging of the evening dimness. What joy to capture a glimmer in a jar! Talk about catching a star! Or three, or twelve.

Later in life, an utterly different circumstance propelled me into creating an adult kind of collection jar—a reflective personal journal— in order to make the most of the new experiences and impressions, to help me not to "waste" or lose them in forgetfulness. After my husband of thirty-two years was diagnosed with lung cancer, our lives became a chaos of tests, surgeries, therapies, tidal waves of pain and relief and anxiety, a roller coaster of emotional highs and lows, prayers, tears, sighs of relief when the results of a particular test were more encouraging than we'd hoped, despondency when the therapies didn't work. I caught all these events, some stars and some starless nights, in my collection jar. We lived day to day, even hour to hour, always on the edge of change and uncertainty.

I realized that I didn't want to lose all this agonizing life-and-death drama in a blur of distorted memories. It all seemed significant, a puzzle with pieces missing, but forming some kind of meaningful pattern we needed to discern. Harold and I both knew that there was much we needed to discover about each other, about mortality, about mystery and transcendence, and about the God we trusted. It's strange how, in the face of terminal illness, one begins to address the existential questions that one has dismissed in an earlier life when the fist of mortality isn't bruising your chin. Crisis times—widowhood, divorce, suicide, job loss, ill health, broken relationships—can become the defining and refining moments of our lives, and unless we achieve a kind of deep honesty with ourselves as flawed, broken people, I'm not sure that we can write with the authenticity that will reach other people where they need to be reached. What we experience and record may well resonate with those we continue to write for. It's a fertile field of stars for the needs of readers.

But during this time of transition, one of my main motivations for the journal was that I wanted our five children, by then nearly all young adults, to read the record of our struggling and questioning, and I wanted them to understand how I was dealing with my own deep inadequacies and frustrations, as well as my efforts to cope and grow and know. Throughout those months, it was not that we found answers to all our queries of the universe, but that we became more aware of the larger patterns of human life and existence, their meaning, or their mystery. The result of this intense, episodic chronicling—more than two years' worth—was eventually whittled down and became a book, *God in the Dark: Through Grief and Beyond,* though at the time of the original writing such editing would have been unthinkable.

I also needed a place where I could vent my overwhelming emotions in privacy. I found that writing out my anguish and bewilderment about my husband's dying and death gave it a name, somehow making it a bit more manageable. I needed to explode on the page when I became rebellious, exhausted, impatient, or just plain angry with God at the unfairness of it all. How could a good and great man like Harold fall victim to lung cancer, a man who never smoked, whose life was given to God's service? How was I going to survive on my own? As I wrote out my inner turmoil, I could say to myself, "Look, there's the pain on the page!" It was no longer churning out of control within me. It had a name and a shape.

For all who are writers, or hope to be, putting emotions into words, even describing them in terms of contours and colors and sensations, will help draw some of the thorns from a wound. And for me, naming the confusion of the mind and heart began to make it seem more manageable. Here's what Simon Brett, in *The Faber Book of Diaries*, says about this kind of attentive writing: "At its simplest, journal-writing is a personal way of imposing some kind of permanence, sanity or order on the chaos of the world around us."

Okay, so we acknowledge the therapeutic value of such a journal. But how might such a notebook benefit the *writer*?

Ron Klug, a master in the world of journal keepers, reassures us in his book, *How to Keep a Spiritual Journal*: "As you write in your journal, you will develop a greater ease and fluency in your writing. This may one day lead you to try writing for publication in a magazine or newspaper, or even to write a book. A journal is a great training ground for the writer, and the experiences and thoughts captured there can be the raw material for many articles and stories." Because new ideas are often as flighty as lightning bugs—little beads of light unpredictably moving in and out of our consciousness—it's vital to record them for future use. When a new concept arrives (writers will often say, "It just came to me," or, "It was borne in upon me that . . . ") we may think,

"Wow. Hmm. A remarkable idea. I doubt if I'll ever forget it," or we'll hear a snatch of conversation, or a descriptive phrase, or the word we've been searching for, waiting to hear, in a poem that fleshes out an essay or story or a poem—some work in progress. Unless we jot it down in an available notebook, though, we may lose the idea as quickly as it came.

"I am new for only a day at a time, like the days on my calendar," I wrote in a journal entry, trying to hold on to the idea as it rushed in. "Or a moment at a time. In a flash the moment is gone, has already grown old and dim—the details fuzzy. I need to capture that moment in its freshness, before its primary insights have evaporated like steam from a wet roof in the sun."

W.H. Auden once asked: "How can I know what I think until I see what I say?" This is a saying much beloved by writing teachers, and I have personally proved its veracity again and again. Once my words are written down in the journal and a train of thought begins, I find it expands and draws other ideas to itself like an enlarging vortex. I learn from the process of writing what I really feel and think. The writing itself begins to teach me.

I have been fascinated to realize, as I write, that the thinking often *follows* or *accompanies* writing rather than preceding it. Poet and essayist Denise Levertov put it like this: "The poet does not see and then begin to search for words to say what he sees: he begins to see and at once begins to say or to sing, and *only in the act of verbalization does he see further*." Elsewhere she tells us, "If one is a poet, then the envisioning, the listening, and the writing of the word are, for that while, fused. . . . In mulling over what I knew I felt and thought, I had stirred up levels of imagination of things I did not know."

In *Reflections on Theological Education,* Henri Nouwen says something similar:

> Most students . . . think that writing means writing down ideas, insights, visions. They feel that they must first have something to say before they

can put it down on paper. For them, writing is little more than recording a pre-existing thought.

But with this approach, true writing is impossible, for *writing is a process in which we discover what lives in us. The writing itself reveals what is alive.* The deepest satisfaction of writing is precisely that it opens up new spaces within us of which we were not aware before we started to write. To write is to embark on a journey whose final destination we do not know. Thus, creative writing requires a real act of trust. We have to say to ourselves, "I do not yet know what I carry in my heart, but I trust that it will emerge as I write." Writing is like giving away the few loaves and fishes one has, trusting that they will multiply in the giving. Once we dare to "give away" on paper the few thoughts that come to us we start discovering how much is hidden underneath . . . and gradually come in touch with our own riches. (emphasis added)

Like Nouwen, many of us experience this eerie sense that, in writing, we are putting down realities we knew already, but that *we never knew we knew.* This suggests that we are in touch with realities beyond us, that we may find ourselves on the edge of mystery, of epiphany. Prayer is part of this procedure, for it works in tandem with the honesty of a journal. Our desire to see, to be attentive to the details of Creation, to be true to what is revealed to us, is a God-given longing.

As we continue to write from that generative place of prayer and that which "we never knew we knew," particularly if we are writing to a specific theme, such as a topical essay, a book review, or a lecture to be prepared for public delivery, we find it astonishing how just about everything we read in magazines or books, or hear in conversation or on the radio, adds in some way to our understanding or contributes a different dimension to what we are writing. Call it serendipity, but if our ears and eyes are open to the vast world of events and ideas, we will find that what we need is available. I call this mechanism the writer's or artist's antenna. And our recording device, our handy journal, allows us to capture this fleeting idea and pin it to the page.

Collector

Such solace at a phrase just written down.
Relief that now it's firmly pinned in place—
an insect stilled that recently had flown
but snagged its wing in this dark brainy space
to be subdued, place marker for collections
of other airborne words, termites or humming bees,
for me to sort and shift and make selections.
When the assortment's fixed the writing flies.

Written in my journal, this brief poem reveals what the process feels like to me. The relieving of the anxiety that comes when we try to carry several significant concepts in our minds at once is a great motivation for keeping a consistent journal, rather than jotting ideas on the backs of envelopes or crumpled receipts or check stubs—for that which is *firmly pinned into place.*

When I put words and ideas onto paper, I discover they begin to gather to themselves more images, more words and ideas. As I write I sometimes have the sensation of joining a stream of enlarging connections, with my pen moving faster and faster to keep up with them. This growing cluster reflects nothing preplanned so much as a kind of organic growth as a seed idea gathers nourishment and sprouts. This is where we can begin to trust the journal process to give our own writing and thinking room to stretch and expand. As Mary Oliver wrote in her poem "The Moths," "If you notice anything / it leads you to notice / more / and more."

Because we may generate many ideas and images in our journals, in our frantic, fragmented world, cluttered with responsibilities that we experience in quick succession without the chance to weigh their meaning, we need to stop and listen to those images and ideas, instead of always compulsively chattering. Though we are often moving too fast to notice it, there is in each of us a profound need to be still, to be alone, to reflect, to meditate, to contemplate, to wait, to reach a kind of bone-deep honesty with our own souls. Keeping a reflective journal takes time, which is a valuable commodity for all of us. The time taken enhances this learning. It compels us to slow down, to decelerate. I like the word *cogitation.* It means "shaking together," which is what our minds do with the thoughts that come and go, given time. A kind of cerebral ballet is performed within our minds if we allow ourselves time to focus and be disciplined.

This slowing down also allows us to pay attention. *Ad-tendere* is the Latin verb "to reach toward." The more I use my journal as a collection jar for my writing, the more I find myself developing the habit of intentionally noticing things—objects, facts, experiences— and describing them in detail, and beyond that, noting my responses to them as part of my journal habit. Remember, in a developing poem or story it's the cogent, concrete details that are the knobs on which the writing hangs, and that create pictures in the readers' minds. If you don't have enough moments during your active day to make extensive notes, simply jot down in your journal some reminder words that will help you to remember later what it was that needed to be further explored.

But beyond a mere record of facts, notes, and events—"lunch with the dean to discuss curriculum," "new grandbaby on the way," "saw deer in the garden again"—the journal records our *responses* to the events and images. As Mary Oliver said in *Owls and Other Fantasies:* "Every day I walk out into the world / to be dazzled, then to be reflective." Naeem Murr admits, ruefully, in a quote on the back cover of *Poetry* magazine: "Poets . . . spend more time 'waiting' than writing . . . twisting the miserable wire coat hanger of their souls this way and that in the hope of becoming more receptive."

Being receptive means receiving the gift that comes from, literally, God knows where. It's a kind of bug hunting with a mental butterfly net provided by the Creator, who gave us imaginations to both capture the seeable for our memory bank and also to see the unseeable.

Often, when I'm reading a novel or magazine article or another writer's poem, or when I'm watching a movie, a word or phrase will jump off the page or screen, and I'll be transfixed. I sense that it is there for me, a small gift that will fill some gap in my own reading or writing or thinking. Into the journal it goes, for future reference, or for a chance to follow that gift, unwinding and examining it more, through time and attention.

But even beyond being a storehouse of ideas and attention, for those of us who are writers, the best benefit of keeping a writer's notebook is that we come to recognize our own distinctive writer's voice, and then to develop, broaden, and enrich it by consistent use. Not only is a journal a place of honest reflection, it is the place for the early creative process to happen or for a project to begin. The creative brainstorming that can happen in a journal gives clarity to what we see in our minds as we learn to focus on the insight of the imagination, learning the best way to express it and then looking back at what we have written or thought and beginning to pull out certain strands, consolidating and reshaping them.

It's a process akin to birthing a child. Kathleen Norris, in *The Quotidian Mysteries,* bemoans the frequent use of birthing as a metaphor for writing, but it's so apt I can't help using it! Many poems and other art forms go through a gestation period. An idea or image may need to "hibernate" for a while to become full-fleshed, ready to face a larger world, which is why it's helpful to reread the journals of the past. Sometimes I'll go on retreat, set up my tent in the wilderness for a couple of days, and follow the trains of thought that flow through the journals of the past months or years. The unsuspected connections I've often made form a pattern or cycle of thinking that can be the foundation for new writing.

My only editors at this primal stage of notation are my own sense of honesty and penetration; the process is worthless without them. For true candor, I must protect the privacy of my thoughts. I even write

"PRIVATE JOURNAL" on the cover of my notebook to guard against peekers and probers, which allows me an odd sense of freedom; because my journal is off-limits to others, it allows me liberty to express what I'm thinking and seeing without risk of offense, misinterpretation, or rebuttal. My confessional. My confidante.

My journal also becomes my training ground, my personal discipline, my companion. It receives whatever I have to give it without complaint or demurral. I was greatly encouraged to hear poet Paul Mariani say, in an almost offhand way, "Your craft is your spiritual discipline." I've never been particularly good at spiritual disciplines—devotional reading and prayer—so this idea, that if I am God-called to be a writer then my writing fulfills this vocation, at least in part, and is pleasing to God and fulfills God's purpose for me, brings me satisfaction. Particularly as I reread past pages, even past journals in their entirety, I gain a sense of momentum, and of a pattern, a larger purpose super-intending my life, even leading me into truths I had been unaware of.

The lessons that my life brings me, asked for or not, catastrophic and excruciating, exhilarating and illuminating, whether I see them coming or not, whether I'm able to encounter them head-on or not, immeasurably enrich and enhance what I have to say, be it in essay, poem, fiction, or creative nonfiction—the larger work that the journal often points to. I love how American writer William Saroyan defined the writer's life—the development of a "rich, immediate, usable past." If we're attentive, the overflow from such a past will keep leaking onto the journal page—a continuing seepage of some consequence. But unless we keep track of those experiences and the lessons derived from them, they won't have the best chance of becoming a part of our ongoing work as writers. Further, since being a writer involves the building of bridges between our own life experience and that of others, our job is to find the most significant points of connection between ourselves and our readers.

While the notes above provide something of the *why* of a writer's journal, let's look toward the practical now, the *what* and *how* of such a notebook.

My own journal writing is decidedly unsystematic. It chronicles things as they occur—quotations, seed poems, diagrams, drawings, movie reviews, book reviews, questions for further consideration, problems, prayers, dreams, visions, insights. I use whatever pen or pencil is handy, but the *actual notebook* is a choice to be carefully considered.

Consider me a thorough-going materialist in my choice of tools. I could use a computer, but the feel of hand-heel and pen on paper and the way the page accepts the words triggers an authentic kind of writing for me. The mechanics of writing down my fleeting thoughts with ease make a difference in how well I record and remember. The actual paper surface (heavy, creamy, and recycled, or skinny and plain for economy or thinness), the pen or pencil—felt-tip, ballpoint, or number-two pencil—such choices will affect the fruitfulness of your journal habit.

My own preference is an unlined journal, because ruled lines feel like *rules* to me (lines are laws, like traffic laws). The word *ruler* comes from the Latin *regulare*—"to regulate," and I want to be independent of such legalisms—free to write or doodle or diagram or sketch or make notes up and down the page instead of across it. This kind of mechanical freedom helps freedom of thought and experiment feel more natural and inevitable to me.

The size is important. If your notebook is to be useful, availability is everything, and that calls for an adjustment according to your habits. Some writers prefer a ring binder so that sheets can be removed and replaced as needed. I prefer a coil-bound booklet that lies flat when open and has sturdy covers because, as my companion, it's likely to get battered as I pluck it from my purse or jam it into a briefcase. A rigid cover makes for a convenient writing surface wherever you are. The choices are so varied these days, in bookstores or gift stores, that it's not hard to find something you'll love, and love to use.

Through carelessness or hurry I have lost several journals (on the seat of a taxi or the front pocket of a plane seat). In each case I lost months of my reflective life and thought. It felt like losing a limb, a part of myself—an arm or a right hand, maybe. My *self*. It's a significant loss. In the last year I've lost notes on a lecture by writer Tom Howard on T.S. Eliot's *Four Quartets* and some priceless (I'm convinced) lines for new poems. I've lost important introductory remarks to a lecture. I've lost a lot of quite private and personal thoughts and opinions. I'm careful, now, to write my name, address, e-mail address, and phone number inside the journal's front cover to make it possible for some conscientious finder to return it to me. Sometimes this works; sometimes it doesn't. I believe my lost journal is orbiting the planet along with socks from the dryer, undelivered letters (with checks), and misdirected luggage. I've learned to let it go. Sigh.

From the choice of journal and paper, pen and pencil, and the return address on the journal, we move to some basics of journal writing, if you need a place to begin.

1. To jump-start your writing when your mind has gone blank, write an answer to one of the following questions: What made me glad today? Or sad? Or mad? Or scared? Remember, in the words of Virginia Hearn: "Nothing *never* happens!"

2. Practice description: How many of your senses are involved in describing the inside of an oyster shell, the skin of a peach, what a summer evening feels like, disappointment at a loss, the look on a stranger's face? Look for the distinctive details that bring your description into sharp focus, and avoid generalizations and abstractions.

3. Describe the writing environment that is most fruitful for you. What feeds and stimulates your creativity? How, or when, do your most creative ideas arrive?

Any of these exercises, performed on any writing surface or computer screen, may prove fruitful. Recorded together in the onward flow of your journal, they represent the path of growth and learning in insight and fluidity and may reveal to you your own unsuspected writing capabilities. As time goes on, you'll find yourself capturing, day after day, the lightning bugs that spark stories, poems, and essays that will make vital connections with your readers.

FURTHER READING

Frederick Buechner, in *Listening to Your Life,* gives a powerful example of the honest self-revelation that has benefited his entire writing life. Natalie Goldberg's *Writing Down the Bones* is one of the classics that has informed and encouraged thousands of journal writers, as is Ronald Klug's *How to Keep a Spiritual Journal.* Emilie Griffin, in *Wilderness Time,* gives a kind of pattern for meditative retreat. Her emphasis on listening, silence, and solitude will support those of us who need to make a deliberate effort to get away from the daily busywork that distracts us from writing creatively. I loved reading Donald Hall's *Life Work,* and learning how this distinguished writer has, over the years, spent his days as a poet and lecturer, and how his environment in New Hampshire has affected his writing habits. Patricia Hampl, in *Virgin Time,* and John Leax, in *Out Walking*, reflect on their creative use of time. In *An Interrupted Life*, Etty Hillesum, a young Dutch woman caught in the Nazi invasion of Holland during World War II, kept her spirit alive by writing her experiences into a journal that was discovered after her death in a Nazi camp. No other writer has written so whimsically as Anne Lamott did in *Bird by Bird*, showing how the daily word-by-word practice of writing can add up to a story, or a book. Back in the seventies I asked Madeleine L'Engle to write a book about how her art and her faith supported and enlarged each other. *Walking on*

Water was the result—still a best seller. Two of my own books came out of my own journal practice—*God in the Dark* was the actual journal I wrote during my husband Harold's cancer and death, full of the existential questions that shake us when we face mortality. And my book *Life Path* is a kind of how-to book for establishing the practice of reflective journal writing.

4

Realms of Gold and Stout Cortez
On Why Writers Ought to Read Widely and Well

Dain Trafton

On First Looking into Chapman's Homer

Much have I travell'd in the realms of gold,
And many goodly states and kingdoms seen;
Round many western islands have I been
Which bards in fealty to Apollo hold.
Oft of one wide expanse had I been told
That deep-brow'd Homer ruled as his demesne:
Yet did I never breathe its pure serene
Till I heard Chapman speak out loud and bold:
Then felt I like some watcher of the skies
When a new planet swims into his ken;
Or like stout Cortez when with eagle eyes
He star'd at the Pacific—and all his men
Look'd at each other with a wild surmise—
Silent upon a peak in Darien.
                                    —John Keats

"Realms of gold"—the rich worlds into which reading leads. Literal realms may be praised as golden—ancient Greece, Renaissance Italy, Elizabethan England—but the metaphor flatters. Sophocles and Michelangelo and Shakespeare lived in the same fallen, tarnished world that we inhabit. You can read about it. Great works of literature—and the other arts, too—are the only way we have to enter realms that always shine. I mean the works themselves, not the states they may describe. The utopia described by Thomas More is not a place I would like to live, but *Utopia* is a place I have never failed to visit with pleasure. The "happy valley" in Dr. Johnson's *Rasselas* is a kind of prison, but *Rasselas* is a liberation.

Sir Philip Sidney, a great poet and novelist, made this fundamental point long ago in *An Apology for Poetry,* a short work of literary theory that sets a standard of style and sense few have met since. By *poetry,* Sidney means all forms of literature, all forms of "making" (the root meaning of *poetry*) in words. "Nature," writes Sidney, "never set forth the earth in so rich a tapestry as divers poets have done. . . . Her work is brazen, the poets only deliver a golden."

When I was a teacher and students asked, "What should I read to help me become a better writer?" I often directed them to "On First Looking into Chapman's Homer." It is a wonderful sonnet— mellifluous, rhythmically seamless, rich with imagery, tightly wrought, intellectually rewarding. Written when Keats was only twenty-one— there's inspiration for you!—it provides a splendid example of what to read and a fascinating lesson in how to read.

"Then felt I . . . like stout Cortez when with eagle eyes / He star'd at the Pacific . . . Silent, upon a peak in Darien." Of course it was Balboa, not Cortez, who was the first European to sight the Pacific, but don't be distracted by that mistake. What you should wonder about is why Keats, the reader who is also a poet, would compare himself to a conquistador, to one of those famously ruthless men who followed Columbus to the New World in order to subdue and plunder it. It's a shocking comparison, one designed to make you think, and it suggests that when you travel in literary realms of gold you must do so not passively, not merely admiring what others have done so well, but rather aggressively, as a kind of conquistador seeking plunder to use in your own work. Like Cortez, you must be "stout"—that is, "proud, fierce, brave, and resolute," to cite that indispensable book for all writers, the *Oxford English Dictionary.* You must be prepared to take from the work of others in constructing your own "demesne," your own island under the aegis of Apollo. You must read with "eagle eyes," with the eyes of a bird of prey. For a writer, Keats implies, that is the beginning of learning to read well.

"On First Looking into Chapman's Homer" is full of the loot that Keats brought back from his own excursion. "Stout," as applied to Cortez, is itself a vivid and memorable description, and it gains force as an allusion to a characteristic device of Homeric style—the heroic epithet: "swift Achilles," "wily Odysseus," "thoughtful Telemachus." And the entire sestet of the sonnet imitates the structure of an epic simile: Ares, the God of War, confronts Diomedes in battle; Diomedes, like a traveler on the bank of a flooded river, turns away; the Myrmidons of Achilles go out to fight like a swarm of bees stirred up by boys. In these and many other ways, Keats's sonnet illustrates how literary allusions or echoes, a kind of literary plunder, can enrich your writing style.

Of course, Homer himself did not disdain such plunder. He took the elements of his style and the matter of his stories, which we now call "Homeric," from a centuries-old oral tradition. Chapman, too, must be considered a kind of conquistador. Translations are at best a kind of noble theft. And Keats, as we have begun to see, took from them both to make a fresh work of his own—subtly stealing from thousands of lines of epic and hundreds of years of literary development to produce fourteen lines of unsurpassed beauty in English. A remarkable feat of literary alchemy.

So, the oral tradition of ancient Greece begat Homer; Homer begat Chapman; and Chapman begat Keats. "No man is an island," wrote John Donne, and neither is any book or play or poem. One of the pleasures of wide and serious reading is the discovery of genealogies of literary inspiration.

Good writing begets good writing—or at least the ambition to write well, and without that ambition, no writer will do the hard work that writing entails. A writer may well ask, who has begotten me as I am today? Whom do I want to beget me as I may become? By reading, you discover your forebears.

I urge you to read as widely as you can, but to travel—for the most part—on the high road of literature. Concentrate on the best writing, the great works from every age and every culture, starting with your own culture and language, whose works you are best equipped to understand, and moving out from there. Learn foreign languages so that you can read as much as possible in the original, but, remembering Keats and Chapman, do not scorn translations. In high school I fell in love with the novels of Dostoevsky as translated with great charm by Constance Garnett. I knew no Russian and rather naïvely assumed that I was reading Dostoevsky himself. Since then, I have heard some rather harsh things said about Garnett's work, but the fact remains that Dostoevsky as she rendered him was a realm of gold for me at a certain point in my life. For lessons in the control of violent shifts of tone, from hilarious satire to the grimmest of horror, you should study her version of Dostoevsky's *The Possessed,* which is perhaps the greatest political novel ever written.

Don't limit yourself to reading only the particular kind of writing you intend to do, or what you find most congenial. Poets should read novels and plays and philosophy and history; novelists should read poetry, and so on. Even if, like the title character in Saul Bellow's *Herzog,* you are considering making a career of writing unsolicited letters to famous people, you will do it better for having read widely and well, for having stayed on the high road. Take to heart the ringing words of Hotspur in Shakespeare's *Henry IV:* "The time of life is short! / To spend that shortness basely were too long."

The high road is easy enough to find—at least in its broad outlines. A good start might be to consult the syllabus of a Great Books course. As a college freshman, I was lucky enough to take such a course, and a splendid journey from high peak to peak it was. The reading for the course included both the *Iliad* and the *Odyssey* (though not in Chapman's translations!), selections from Thucydides' *History of the Peloponnesian War,* Sophocles' *Oedipus the King,* Plato's *Apology of Socrates,* the biblical book of Job, selections from Livy's *History of Rome,* Virgil's *Aeneid,* Dante's *Inferno,* selections from Chaucer's *Canterbury Tales,* Shakespeare's *King Lear,* Milton's *Paradise Lost,* Swift's *Gulliver's Travels,* Stendhal's *The Red and the Black,* Flaubert's *Madame Bovary,* and Dickens's *Bleak House.*

Here are some realms of gold every writer should eagle-eye, but keep in mind that they are just a beginning, just the outskirts of the New World. Having read Homer and Virgil, move on to the epics of other traditions, *Gilgamesh,* the *Mahabharata, Beowulf.* To Thucydides and Livy, add Herodotus and later works such as Machiavelli's *Discourses,* Gibbon's *Decline and Fall of the Roman Empire,* and Francis Parkman's *Montcalm and Wolfe* (a masterpiece about American history by a great American historian). After Stendhal, Flaubert, and Dickens, turn to Tolstoy, Jane Austen, and George Eliot: *Anna Karenina, Emma,* and *Middlemarch* are milestones on the literary high road.

Read all of Dante, not just the *Inferno,* which is the perennial favorite because—or so people say—evil is more interesting than good. This is all the more reason to study the *Purgatorio (Purgatory)* and the *Paradiso (Heaven),* the latter of which, to my taste, contains the highest reaches of Dante's poetic achievement. Do you want to know how to make goodness shine with the beauty it deserves—that is, without the sentimentality that so often vitiates the representation of goodness in art? If so, study the *Paradiso's* paean to Beatrice, Dante's lost love, with whom he is reunited in heaven. (I strongly recommend reading the *Divine Comedy* in the translation by Dorothy Sayers and Barbara Reynolds, available in paperback. Its extremely helpful introductions and notes are a liberal education in themselves.)

Read as much Chaucer as you can. And as much Milton, too. Travel beyond *Paradise Lost* to *Paradise Regained, Comus* (Milton's pastoral play or "masque"), *Areopagitica* (his famous argument in favor of an unlicensed press), and "Lycidas"—especially "Lycidas," which in spite of Dr. Johnson's myopic strictures in his *Lives of the Poets,* deserves a place beside Shakespeare's and Keats's lyrics on the very summit of Parnassus. "Lycidas" is not an easy read for contemporaries, but the challenge is well worth taking up. As the Miltonic diction and syntax become familiar, the poem's rhythm and melody—its song—will carry you away. There is no more moving celebration of God's grace than this meditation on a death that seems untimely and incomprehensible, and yet is redeemed:

> *So Lycidas, sunk low, but mounted high,*
> *Through the dear might of him that walked the waves,*
> *Where other groves and other streams along,*
> *With nectar pure his oozy locks he laves,*
> *And hears the unexpressive nuptial song,*
> *In the blest kingdoms meek of joy and love.*
> *There entertain him all the saints above,*
> *In solemn troops, and sweet societies*
> *That sing, and singing in their glory move,*
> *And wipe the tears for ever from his eyes.*

Whether you write poetry or prose, the noble harmony of this language, whose very flow seems to constitute a promise of the divine mercy it describes, should be an inspiration and an example. Modern and contemporary literature, apparently so antithetical to so much of what Milton stands for, is nonetheless full of his influence—in Eliot, in Faulkner, in Robert Lowell, in Richard Wilbur. Perhaps, if you make the effort to steep yourself in his high achievements, you will find his effects in you.

No writer in any language has a higher fame than Shakespeare, and the more you read him with eagle eyes the more you will discover how fully he deserves his reputation. There is no kind of making with words that Shakespeare has not mastered. If you want to inform your sensibility with the full range of expressiveness in English, you must study the "infinite variety" (Enobarbus's encomium on Cleopatra) of Shakespearean language in tragedy, comedy, history, and in his sonnets. If you want to understand how to give even minor characters complexity and depth by a few deft touches, you should pay close attention to Bottom and his fellow craftsmen in *A Midsummer Night's Dream,* to the citizens in *Coriolanus,* to the murderers in *Macbeth,* to Polonius in *Hamlet.* If you want to know how to construct a beginning, a middle, and an end—the three parts of a dramatic action as defined by Aristotle in the *Poetics*—you should examine the making of Shakespeare's plots. What more brilliant opening, for example, than the scene of storm and shipwreck in *The Tempest?* "What cheer?" asks the boatswain in the fearsome storm; "Where's the master?" asks the King of Naples. These questions prefigure the action of the entire play. What more tragically satisfying ending than *King Lear*'s, which leaves all in doubt but convinces us there is nothing more to say?

Of course you should know the Bible through and through. As the Word of God, how can it not be a resource for writers of faith? I understand the complaints about academic courses on "the Bible as literature," but it *is* great literature, the most wonderful collection of stories ever assembled. The Creation, Cain and Abel, Abraham and Isaac, David and Goliath, David and Bathsheba, Elijah and the chariot of fire, the birth of Jesus, the raising of Lazarus, Judas, the crucifixion, the resurrection and ascension—every writer should be familiar with these narratives, which have been retold and reworked through the ages, sometimes in subtle and almost unrecognizable ways. You should consider how you can retell them too, perhaps with only the deftest of allusions to the Bible. (Whatever your favorite translation, you should be familiar with the the King James Version, whose language, though archaic in places, is both grand and subtle, and has a peculiar resonance because of its influence on generations of great writers from Milton to the present.)

"Call me Ishmael," says Herman Melville's narrator at the beginning of *Moby Dick*, which is probably the great American novel that some dream still needs writing. At the heart of this book is a reenactment of the great biblical pattern of sin and redemption (with a strong emphasis on sin), told in a language stolen boldly from the Bible. The hymn that "swelled high above the howling of the storm" in Father Mapple's chapel in New Bedford before Ishmael embarks turns out to be a very free adaptation of the eighteenth Psalm. The final chapter begins with words taken from the messengers of ill tidings in Job. I once taught a seminar in which we read *Moby Dick, King Lear,* and *Paradise Lost* in the context of selected biblical passages. It was an education in creative writing to contemplate the noble plunder on which those works were built.

It is said that the principal source of Abraham Lincoln's education was the Bible, the only book his frontier family owned. Yet Lincoln is perhaps our only president who deserves to be ranked among the truly great writers. He read the Bible in log cabins in Kentucky and Indiana (by firelight, so the story goes), in his law office in Illinois, and in the White House. Its spirit and language informed his eloquence with both sternness and compassion—with the courage (including a degree of hardness) that it took to lead the country into war and with the pity that he characteristically expressed for its victims, including those in the South who were in some degree the victims of his own hardness. "The Almighty has His own purposes," he wrote in his second inaugural address. "Woe unto the world because of offenses, for it must needs be that offenses come; but woe unto the man by whom the offense cometh!" And then: "With malice toward none; with charity for all; with firmness in the right, as God gives us to see the right, let us strive on to finish the work we are in; to bind up the nation's wounds; to care for him who shall have borne the battle, and for his widow, and his orphan—to do all which may achieve and cherish a just, and a lasting peace, among ourselves, with all nations."

So, filling his hearers' ears with words and cadences of what still counted as *the* Book for our troubled nation, Lincoln made literary gold out of a brazen reality. Such rhetoric can still play a role in our public life, as the speeches and sermons of Martin Luther King Jr. and others demonstrate.

The literary high road is the surest route to realms of gold, but there are byways and lanes worth exploring too. One that has been valuable to a current project of mine (a collection of stories set in colonial New England) is Cotton Mather's *Magnalia Christi Americana* (*The Great Deeds of Christ in America*), the quintessentially Puritan commentary on the early settlement, controversies, and wars of Massachusetts and surrounding colonies. Believe it or not, Mather can be a very lively writer. His style—a mixture of Latinate formality and down-to-earth Anglo-Saxon directness—proves to be a perfect medium for expressing the Puritans' deeply ambivalent experience of their New World in the wilderness. Anyone interested in understanding early America from the European point of view should get to know Mather. (The *Magnalia* is still in print and available in paperback.)

Even the subliterary can have charms for a writer—especially one with a satiric bent. In *The Praise of Folly,* Erasmus extracted gold from the cultural dregs of the late Middle Ages, satirizing the rhetoric of self-serving politicians, the pomposity of school teachers, the obfuscations of lawyers. John Dryden did something similar in *MacFlecknoe,* a hilarious send-up of bad poetry at the end of the seventeenth century. A few years later, Alexander Pope, brilliantly appropriating and transforming *MacFlecknoe,* produced his more general dissection of intellectual perversion in *The Dunciad.*

Flannery O'Connor, forced by ill health to live with her mother in Milledgeville, Georgia, recorded the absurdities of local culture in her letters and in her fiction. To the poets Robert Lowell and Elizabeth Hardwick, she sent the following Mother's Day poem that she had heard "Senator Pappy Daniels" read on the radio: "I had a mother. I had to have. I lover whether she's good or bad. I lover whether she's live or dead. Whether she's an angel or an old dope head." This poem, in its sublime awfulness, is precisely the sort of material O'Connor specialized in raising to the level of high art in her fiction. There are riches all around you.

Ars longa, vita brevis. The time of life is short, the time for reading and writing even shorter—far too short to travel the high road to the end, much less to venture down all its interesting byways. The recommendations in this essay and in the appended reading list are meant to be suggestive, not definitive, certainly not exhaustive. You must make your own list, following your own tastes and building your own course for lifelong learning in great (and lesser) books. If your experience is anything like mine, you are bound to find that your list grows faster than you can read the works on it, which can be discouraging or exhilarating, depending on your point of view. I tend towards exhilaration as I contemplate the realms of gold stretched out before me, and I hope you will too. Is there anything more pleasant than reading, and especially reading with the eagle eyes of the writer, gazing on new worlds with a wild surmise?

As for me, a man not far from completing his allotted three score and ten, the evident impossibility of reading and writing as much as I want to in this life leads me sometimes to wonder whether those activities will exist in heaven. According to Dante's *Paradiso* and the great eschatological tradition on which it draws, the saved in heaven devote themselves solely and utterly to praising God. But could this mean something other than infinite iterations of the doxology? Keats's "On First Looking into Chapman's Homer" reminds us of the long tradition that finds something of the Divine in the experience of great literature; reading gives us a breath of the "pure serene." And Milton tells us that the dead Lycidas, who was a writer, hears "the unexpressive nuptial song," and is entertained by "all the Saints above," who "sing, and singing in their glory move." Like a king in Homeric days, the Lycidas in heaven listens to songs that console him.

Presumably, he will learn by listening and begin to sing himself. I don't want to push this little flight of fancy too far, but Dante and Keats and Milton, not to mention a host of others, suggest that imagining the life to come is not necessarily a vain and illegitimate undertaking—provided, of course, we undertake it with proper respect and modesty. Whether the saved praise God in heaven by reading (or listening) and writing (or singing) must remain a matter of doubt, but I consider it a kind of piety to entertain the possibility. Could it be that the intense joy that we can find through immersion in those creative activities on Earth provides a foretaste of what we will experience in the presence of God?

FURTHER READING

Many interesting and useful case studies can be devised to illustrate the ways in which writers profit creatively from their reading. Here are a few examples:

Virgil's *Aeneid* is a great poem in its own right, and it is also a fascinating example of Virgil's transformation of earlier material—in this case, Homer's *Iliad* and *Odyssey*. The three poems should be read together, with an eye to Virgil's deep departures from (as well as his obvious fidelity to) his Homeric models. From the same point of view, it is also worth considering later imitations of Homer, including two distinctively modern adaptations: James Joyce's *Ulysses* and Nikos Kazantzakis's *The Odyssey: A Modern Sequel.* Virgil, Joyce, and Kazantzakis are first-class literary plunderers.

So is Shakespeare. I recommend reading the Roman plays—*Julius Caesar, Antony and Cleopatra,* and *Coriolanus*—in the light of the appropriate sections of Plutarch's *Lives of the Noble Grecians and Romans.* Shakespeare used the lively Elizabethan translation of

Plutarch by Sir Thomas North, sometimes following its language very closely while introducing touches of psychological and intellectual complexity that help to define the quality that we think of as essentially Shakespearean.

Ben Jonson is one of the finest of English lyric poets. In the seventeenth century he inspired a group of followers known as the "Sons of Ben," who rivaled John Donne and the "Metaphysicals" in style and wit. One of the best of the Sons of Ben was Robert Herrick, who sometimes imitated his model almost to the point of plagiarism, but with brilliant results. Compare Herrick's famous "Delight in Disorder" with Jonson's "Song" that begins "Still to be neat, still to be drest, / As you were going to a feast." You will see how, through the slightest and subtlest of refinements, the son created new gold out of old, and (in my opinion) outdid the father.

It was as a reader of *Beowulf* and *Sir Gawain and the Green Knight* that I first (years ago) encountered the scholarly and critical work of J.R.R. Tolkien—especially his famous essay "*Beowulf*: the Monsters and the Critics." Writers who love Tolkien's fiction will find this essay well worth reading. And of course they will find it valuable to explore the medieval literature that he plundered to create the magical world of his imagination. The works of C.S. Lewis and Dorothy Sayers offer similar examples of the ways in which scholarly research can enrich writing.

5

Getting It Right
On Research

Rudy Nelson

It's a beautiful spring day in the comic strip world of Calvin and Hobbes, but Calvin is down in the dumps:

> Calvin: I've got to write a report for school.
> Hobbes: What's the topic?
> Calvin: Bats. Can you imagine anything more stupid? (Shifting into high dudgeon.) Heck, I don't know anything about bats! How am I supposed to write a report on a subject I know nothing about?! It's impossible!
> Hobbes: I suppose research is out of the question.
> Calvin: Oh, like I'm going to learn about bats and **then** write a report?! Give me a break!

While it's Hobbes's calm voice of reason we all identify with here, I have to admit that on occasion I've felt more than a little bit like Calvin—facing a writing task on a subject I know nothing about and not sounding hallelujahs at the prospect of buckling down to the difficult business of research. But Calvin's no dummy. He'll get over his tantrum after a while and he'll probably do a pretty good paper on bats. And some years down the road he may even discover (though knowing Calvin, I wouldn't bet the farm on it) that the actual and potential rewards of research and writing are worth the commitment of a whole life.

As writing partners over the years, Shirley Nelson and I have always been careful to identify ourselves as storytellers, perhaps as a safety measure, a rationale for meandering restlessly across the genres. The core of any of our work has always been story, though the context might be history or biography or journalism, and the medium print or film. But storytelling has not excused us from the necessity of research, even when fiction itself has been the focus. Again and again we've found ourselves moving blindly into new territory, asking a thousand questions (many of them naïve), falling into unexpected discoveries, and picking ourselves up from mistakes.

A recently completed major project, our documentary film, *Precarious Peace: God and Guatemala,* is an example of that kind of adventure, and a good place to begin this discourse, since it represents our most compete collaboration as researchers.

Starting from Scratch—or Otherwise

It's not that we lacked background as a launching point. We began research specifically for the film in 1998. Like the majority of North Americans, a dozen years earlier we could barely locate Guatemala on a map, given the media's slim and erratic coverage of all things Central American. But then I made my first trip to Central America in the summer of 1987 and, in the decade between 1987 and 1998, returned four more times. Moreover, our deep concerns over the problematic involvement of the United States in Central America had already stimulated a serious effort to understand how five hundred years of territorial and economic colonialism and militarism had led to the present situation. So when the actual film project began in 1998, we had a semblance of knowledge to build on.

Actually, we've never begun any project in a vacuum. For *The Last Year of the War,* Shirley's novel about a young girl's experience at a fictional Bible Institute in Chicago during the final year of World War II, she was able to draw not only on her conversion as a teenager and her experience in the evangelical subculture but on eight months as a Moody Bible Institute student in the same year as her book's action was cast. My undergraduate philosophy major, seminary education at Boston University School of Theology, and doctoral program in American Civilization at Brown (including a concentration in American religious history), gave me the temerity to tackle an intellectual biography of Edward John Carnell, the leading philosopher-theologian of the midcentury evangelical renaissance. And for Shirley's history of an authoritarian Christian group in southern Maine—*Fair, Clear, and Terrible: The Story of Shiloh, Maine*—she had an inexhaustible supply of stories from her mother and father, who grew up in that perfectionist community as children and then defected as young adults.

But however valuable personal experience may be as a head start, it has always quickly led us into unexplored locations. And that's the safest place to be. For research to be done from the right perspective, it's best to consider yourself a blank tablet. That was certainly true as we braved the subject of Guatemala.

Boundaries

A friend who recently heard that I was working on an essay about research suggested that the text of the entire piece consist of a single word: *Google*. Kidding or not, he had a point. While for 90 percent of our writing careers the word *google* represented nothing more than the babbling of an infant in a bassinette, we've come to appreciate in recent years how it has put at our fingertips, all day, every day, a virtual world-class library in whose stacks we can wander at will. But as every researcher learns sooner or later, this easy access is a mixed blessing.

In this era of information overload, we should all be humming the song "It Ain't Necessarily So" in the back of our minds as we cruise the Internet for information. Moreover, as one Google entry leads to another and another and yet another, one has to decide when the search has gotten out of hand. When only two roads diverge in the woods, one might reasonably decide (contra Robert Frost) to try them both. But when there are dozens of side roads, it's time to get your choices under control.

It's often not easy to set boundaries for our research tasks. In his book *The Landscape of History: How Historians Map the Past,* John Lewis Gaddis gives an illustration meant primarily for historians but clearly applicable to research in other genres:

> It would make no sense, for example, to begin an account of the Japanese attack on Pearl Harbor with the launching of the planes from their carriers: you'd want to know how the carriers came to be within range of Hawaii, which requires explaining why the government in Tokyo chose to risk war with the United States. But you can't do that without discussing the American oil embargo against Japan, which in turn was a response to the Japanese takeover of French Indochina. Which of course resulted from the opportunity provided by France's defeat at the hands of Nazi Germany, together with the frustrations Japan had encountered in trying to conquer China. Accounting for all of this, however, would require some attention to the rise of authoritarianism and militarism during the 1930s, which in turn had something to do with the Great Depression as well as the perceived inequities of the post–World War I settlement, and so on. You could continue this process all the way back to the moment, hundreds of millions of years earlier, when the first Japanese island rose up, in great billowing clouds of steam and smoke, from what was to become the Pacific Ocean. However, we don't usually go back quite that far.

That's enough to give a researcher a severe case of vertigo. But if "we don't usually go back quite that far," how far back *should* we go? Or, depending on the subject, how far *in*? How far *afield*? The answer will depend on the purpose of the project, and that may develop only as the research continues.

So when should research stop and writing begin? In our view, it's wrong—and dangerous—to even ask such a question. That way of thinking is responsible for hundreds of PhDs that were never awarded because the research went on interminably and actual writing never got off the ground. Those two parts of the creative process should walk hand in hand from start to finish. In this regard, film is no different from any print genre. Whether creating fiction, nonfiction, theatre, or film, the production cycle requires vision, planning, shaping, and research to one extent and another. And every one of these involvements is part of the writing process. If we had dichotomized research and production on *Precarious Peace*—delaying the start of production until all the research was completed—the film would never have been made. To be sure, at first there was a heavy balance on research. We had a lot of reading to do. Robert Stone, whose novel *A Flag for Sunrise* captures the insidious threat of violence in Central America during the 1970s, says that a novelist who deals with moral and political dimensions must assume, above all, "*the responsibility to understand.* The novel that admits to a political dimension requires a knowledge . . . intuitive or empirical, of the situation that is its subject." (emphasis added)

Our project was not fiction, which put us even more under the onus of getting the facts straight. The "responsibility to understand," involved not just the five hundred–year culture of violence that is the country's history—including the thirty-six-year civil war that had been brought to an end in 1996—but the thorny issues of religion as well, as clearly indicated in the film's subtitle, *God and Guatemala.* Christianity in Guatemala arrived hand in hand with violence in the Spanish invasion of the New World and has been entangled with the forces of domination ever since. As our research continued, we discovered that no missionaries to Guatemala, from the Spanish Roman Catholic clergy of the sixteenth century to the Protestant educators and Pentecostal evangelists of the twentieth, have been able to escape the shadow of violence. On the other hand, there has always been within the country's religious communities a creative minority that has worked for freedom and justice. These are subtle and complex issues, and late in 2002—four years after our starting point—we were still doing research that added to our understanding even as the cinematic components headed off to the lab for their final editing.

Research into story also continued deep into the production schedule. As Sandra Cisneros says in her foreword to Virgilio Elizondo's *The Future Is Mestizo,* "It is always, after all, about telling stories, stories that save our lives." And in Guatemala, there was no shortage of stories that would make great narrative history for a documentary. Our first tentative format was a trio of reports about U.S. citizens who were in Guatemala for very different purposes—a cultural anthropologist, a Methodist schoolteacher, and a Roman Catholic missionary—all three targeted as suspicious by the Guatemalan military government, with their lives and work in imminent danger. These were riveting and important stories, but they were about North Americans. So, after working on that approach for a year, we abandoned it with regret and continued the search. We had compiled many disparate parts of a potential documentary, some thirty tapes of footage, hours of screening time, that sat on the shelves of our workroom, but we still didn't have the right story that would tie these parts together and open windows to the role of religion in Guatemala's past, present, and future. It was late fall 2001, three full years after beginning work on the film, that we found the right story—a Mayan family, three surviving sisters and their father, who had lost many members of their extended family in a massacre in the war's worst period in 1981 and were now rebuilding their lives in the postwar period. Like most Guatemalans, they had kept silent for twenty years in fear of retaliation, but they were now willing to talk on camera. The continuing search for the right story had finally paid off. The three Atz sisters and their father gave us what we were waiting for.

Roadblocks

There will be roadblocks in the course of any research. And some of them are bound to be serious. One year after Catherine Drinker

Bowen had begun her biography of Oliver Wendell Holmes, she was told that Holmes's two literary executors had chosen someone to write the *definitive* biography, that all written materials were reserved for that project, and that, therefore, she could not use any data from the letters that she had already been allowed to see. This prohibition meant that if she were to include any fact that she had gleaned from that research she would have to verify it independently from someone who could personally testify to it. To be sure, there was a silver lining to that cloud. From her work in the letters she at least knew what facts she would be seeking to corroborate. Bowen persisted and found a way around the roadblock, and *Yankee from Olympus,* her Holmes biography, was eventually published by Atlantic Monthly Press. With occasional exceptions—for example, the key person who refuses to be interviewed under any conditions—there is always a way around roadblocks. Still, it's not pleasant for a researcher to be clobbered on the head with the word *definitive.*

In my research for *The Making and Unmaking of an Evangelical Mind: The Case of Edward Carnell,* I soon confronted a completely unexpected impasse. I had the family's promise of cooperation and permission to look at personal records. But I discovered that no collection of Carnell papers existed. Shortly after Edward Carnell died, his widow sold the family home, gave away his books and his opera recordings, and (with one or two exceptions) destroyed all his correspondence and personal papers—not for any dark conspiratorial reason, not to hide embarrassing material, but simply because she assumed that none of this would be of value to anyone.

After absorbing that bad news, I realized that the written records from Carnell's five-year presidency of Fuller Seminary would take on added importance. But I was astonished to find that the seminary had no files of such material. I had rather good evidence that I was not being stonewalled by the administration, because they gave me a key to a basement storeroom where scores of boxes with hard-copy files were kept, and the unsupervised freedom to examine and use anything I found. There was an abundance of interesting and significant material, some of it quite sensitive, but almost nothing from the Carnell presidency.

There's a second part to this story, and in an essay on research, I have to admit it's a bit embarrassing. A few years later, still at work on the book, having read and reread all of Carnell's published writings, having amassed much documentary material, having interviewed Carnell's family, students, colleagues, friends, and others, but still regretful at the absence of crucial correspondence, I got a letter from historian George Marsden, who had begun work on a history of Fuller Seminary and who knew of the serious gap in primary sources related to Carnell's presidency. In the attic of the Hamilton, Massachusetts, home of Harold John Ockenga, Fuller's first president, Marsden had discovered an entire file of correspondence between Carnell and Ockenga. This was great news. A day poring over those letters in the Ockenga attic provided much valuable information and a deeply personal dimension that wouldn't have been otherwise present in the book. What's embarrassing is that a year before Marsden's discovery I had interviewed Ockenga in that very house and failed to ask the simple direct question that might have led to the vital cache of correspondence in the attic.

Grace Notes

After chipping into the cup from a sand trap and being told he was lucky, Jack Nicklaus, the greatest golfer of his generation, said, "Right. But I notice that the more I practice, the luckier I get."

And so it is with the totally unexpected discoveries that serendipitously inject excitement and reward into the research process. More often than not they come during the equivalent of a Nicklaus practice session, hitting a hundred golf balls out of a dozen sand traps from various angles and distances.

Our big lucky break in the *Precarious Peace* research was coming across what journalists would call a scoop: an account of a back-channel series of efforts that culminated in a secret March 1990 conference in Oslo, Norway, involving representatives of the Guatemalan government, the military, and the guerrillas. That conference turned out to be the first definitive step in a process that culminated six years later in the signing of peace accords bringing an official end to the thirty-six-year civil war. By the time we started our research, the Oslo conference was part of the official record, but the process that led up to it was virtually unknown. We stumbled on the story by patiently following leads as they came to our attention. At the end of one particular trail we found Paul Wee, a Lutheran clergyman. The Reverend Doctor Wee, at the time an executive with Lutheran World Federation, had come to know and respect some of the self-exiled Guatemalan guerrilla leaders in Geneva, Switzerland, where his office was located. When he and Phil Anderson, another Lutheran clergyman, were unexpectedly granted an interview with the top man in the Guatemalan military, they sensed a rare opportunity to jumpstart a peace process that had begun a few years earlier but had come to a standstill. With the permission of the various peace groups, they presented a question to the general. If a conference were set up in a neutral location, with no press coverage and no cost to the participants, would he be willing to send delegates to sit down and talk with the guerrilla leaders? Since all previous efforts to set up similar conferences had failed, Wee and Anderson were stunned when, this time, the general, after briefly consulting with his aides, agreed to the conditions. The conference went off without a hitch, Wee was present for all the sessions, and his account of the proceedings, especially the extraordinary final session, is a high point of the film.

In the late sixties, when Shirley began researching the history of Shiloh, the closed community in southern Maine, she had no idea she was doing anything more than helping her father write his memoirs. One of the anecdotes she had heard repeatedly regarded her mother's brother Leander, who had died at Shiloh at age fourteen. Disturbing circumstances surrounded his death, but were never fully explained, except to say that the boy had planned to run away and was stricken with diphtheria before he could do so.

In the face of a massive and possibly obtuse history, Leander became for Shirley a living, red-blooded focus of the search. If no other significant data should present itself, here was a story to pursue and tell, worthwhile in itself. To her surprise, she found it quickly, on microfilm, in the basement of the Bowdoin College library, the lead story on the front page of the local newspaper, January 23, 1904. "The Charge Is Manslaughter" read the headline. The leader of the Shiloh community, Frank W. Sandford, was being charged with negligence in the death of Leander Bartlett. This, as it turned out, was the first of three manslaughter trials involving Sandford that would eventually shape the book, *Fair, Clear, and Terrible: The Story of Shiloh, Maine,* published twenty years after that first research discovery. The dedication reads: "For Leander, who almost got away."

Fact and Fiction

Barbara Kingsolver, drawing on her experience working in different genres, once said, "Write a nonfiction book, and be prepared for the legion of readers who are going to doubt your facts. But write a novel, and get ready for the world to assume that every word is true." The implication, of course, is that in fiction not every word is "true." In the imagined world the novelist has created, verisimilitude—the literal factual equivalency of that imagined world to the external world of our daily lives—is often in short supply. But that doesn't mean anything goes. As Kingsolver would be the first to admit, fiction explores a far deeper and more important level of *truth* than verisimilitude can touch.

We've been dealing with the issue of truth in fiction in our current project—a novel that started out as a nonfiction book. The concept of the book began as a multigenerational account of a pioneer missionary family: what kind of lives did the missionary children of the next two generations live? After months of initial research combing through a variety of sources, looking for a family that fulfilled the necessary criteria, every likely candidate fell short in one way or another. I can still remember the exact moment, walking home from the university one afternoon in 1990, when the right question finally came to mind: why don't we *create* a missionary family that meets our specifications and tell their story in a novel? That solved one problem and introduced many others. The setting of the novel, as in our documentary film, is Guatemala, with its continuing culture of violence. The question that troubled us was how to represent the true breadth of that culture accurately.

When Chilean author Ariel Dorfman, persona non grata in his own country, wished to write a novel about the practice under the Pinochet regime of making enemies of the state "disappear," he knew there was no way it could be published in Chile. So he developed an elaborate strategy to circumvent the inevitable ban. He moved the time back to World War II and the locale to Denmark under Nazi occupation. Writing under the pseudonym Eric Lohmann, supposedly a Danish writer who completed the novel just before he was taken away by the gestapo, Dorfman added a final touch, transferring the action to a country resembling Greece. Further distancing from Pinochet's Chile was created by the ruse that the manuscript had lain hidden for thirty years before Lohmann's family discovered and published it. All this was to make it possible for the book to be published in Chile without getting author and publisher thrown in jail and perhaps executed. When the publisher got cold feet and backed out of the deal, Dorfman decided that by using this strategy of disguise he had struck a universal note; he went ahead with the original plan. The result is the novel *Widows,* published simultaneously in the United States and Canada in 1983.

What's the connection to our novel? Even with its setting in the violent context of Guatemala, if and when our novel is published, neither authors nor publisher will risk jail time. But the problems in writing and research are comparable. Dorfman struck the "universal note" by removing the novel's story from the actual situation in Chile and trusting the reader to make the connection. Our novel has to take place in a literal Guatemala in three distinct and recognizable time frames: 1954, 1987, and the present—that is, the moment it is in the hands of the reader. And, because in each of those periods the fictional characters are interacting with real historical situations, the larger truths—the universal values that are our deeper objective—must have an organic connection with the real country of Guatemala. We've set the authenticity bar high, and that means the commensurate demands of research are formidable.

Considering the rigorous demands of research, lasting for years in some writing projects, it's understandable why writers sometimes feel they should get more credit for doing it. The Along Publishers Row section in the Winter 2007 issue of *Authors Guild Bulletin* points out that the recent trend of some novelists to include a bibliography is generating a bit of controversy. Is it a genuine effort to give credit where credit is due or an ostentatious display of learning? I won't comment on that question, except to ask if anyone interested in the art and craft of writing ever seriously doubted that novelists do research, often just as much as a nonfiction author. And while, particularly in recent years, it is generally recognized that, with some notable exceptions, the full range of fictional techniques is available to the nonfiction writer, we do well to heed literary journalist John McPhee's warning that to confuse the two genres violates the contract with the reader.

The fact that, as storytellers, we have worked in several genres does not relax one bit either the commitment to conscientious research or the integrity with which the resources are handled. Whether novelists, biographers, investigative journalists, or card-carrying historians, writers of faith owe it to our readers and our subject—to the high calling of the search for truth—to commit ourselves to whatever level of research is necessary to get it right.

But while getting it right is a useful standard, it bears a necessary subtext. However impressive the range of our research, however conscientious our handling of the mountain of materials, we will not have the last word. Somewhere down the road, new evidence will turn up. Or a writer with a different set of conceptual tools will look at the same evidence and tell it a different way. History will always be rewritten. Recognizing that inevitability in the future in no sense lessens the mandate on us in the present.

FURTHER READING

For guidance in all aspects of basic research, two excellent resources are *The Craft of Research*, 2nd edition, edited by Wayne Booth, Gregory Columbo, and Joseph Williams, and *The New York Public Library Book of How and Where to Look It Up*, Sherwood Harris, editor-in-chief. Continuing conscientious exposure to the research experiences of other writers can vicariously widen one's own ability to track down information and improvise solutions to unexpected problems. At certain points in my own work, I've found Barbara Tuchman's *Practicing History: Selected Essays* and James Clifford's *From Puzzles to Portraits: Problems of a Literary Biographer* especially helpful.

6

A Twitch Upon the Thread
On Writing as an Act of Faith

Emilie Griffin

When I was eleven, I decided to be a writer. No doubt that was because I loved stories and poems. But also I loved (as I still do) to pick up a soft, dark pencil or a quick-flowing pen and watch words spill across a ruled sheet of paper, feeling the flex of a notebook, enjoying the smooth skin of loose-leaf paper. I loved the act of writing; not those seventh-grade book reports and class assignments, but my *own* writing, writing that expressed my heartfelt desire.

One day I invited my mother and father into the dining room. I had something important to read to them. It was a story I had written myself in a black-and-white, mottled-cover composition book. The story was written in pencil on wide-ruled pages; it was a story about horses. I was lost in a storybook world of dogs, horses, and ponies. These were not just animal stories, mind you, but stories of courage, adventure, and risk. What I loved to read became what I wanted to write.

I felt called to write. Writing was my gift, my talent, my identity.

Wasn't this call like the Bible story of young Samuel in the temple, when he heard a voice calling his name and did not know it was God? I suspect so. Yet, what happened was no more than an inkling (not a voice heard even internally but an urge), something that prompted me, indicating the path.

This was not a voice such as the prophets heard, in which God gave definite instructions, what to do, how to save the people, where to go, what to say to Pharaoh when the time came. No, definitely not.

Instead, I felt a gentle pull (what English writer Evelyn Waugh calls "a twitch upon the thread") and the hush of an invitation, like the low door in *Alice in Wonderland,* or the small bottle that says, "Drink me."

When I was as young as eleven, did I really think I had been summoned? Not likely. But I felt the pull. I recognized myself in Samuel's story. Samuel and David and Daniel were my favorite Bible people—because they were called. God spoke to them and had in mind something for them to do. Sometimes they were even anointed with oil.

Samuel and David were called. I was called. I was meant to do something. Some inner voice said, "Write!" just as God's voice commanded, "Write!" in the book of the prophet Habakkuk:

> Write the vision down
> inscribe it on tablets
> to be easily read;
> since this vision is for its own time only.

When a voice comes so insistently, we want to do what is asked of us, yet we are not sure. If we are wise, we run from self-delusion, from grandiose thinking or arrogance. We wait for confidence, for clarity. We listen for the questions. We write our way through them. And sometimes we wait.

Besides this inner calling is also a calling from outside, from those who see talent in us: teachers, parents, friends. "Maybe you will be a poet or write a book some day." Random affirmations and compliments from these observers strike home. "I am a writer," says the voice within. "Yes, I am a writer. I will write." Inwardly, we are glad to find out who we are and dream of what we might express, and this recognition is freeing, as in Emily Dickinson's line: "At last, to be identified!"

Not every writer would conceive of this impulse to write in terms of calling or vocation. Even some Christian writers would speak about compulsion, a relentless drive. Still, something pushes us to write. Otherwise, we could not take the pressure and stay the course.

Till now I have been speaking of a writer's early formation, when everything seems lighted up by grace. Words fall easily from the pen. Consolation comes often: early successes in student days, the essay prize, the short story award, first publication in a school magazine. Yet, like Milton's leaves of Vallombrosa, these honors skitter away, becoming faded memories.

That is when the real challenge begins. After the high enthusiasm of first submissions to major publications or publishers, after we have grasped our calling, then we attempt the real work of faith. By "faith" I do not mean only a writer's assent to a variety of religious beliefs and precepts. Instead, I mean what is described in the letter to the Hebrews: "the substance of things hoped for, the evidence of things not seen." The writer must describe a world infused by God with meaning, a world undergirded by God's grace. For God is the one who gives us the insight and vision to make a work of art. Surely the faith of a writer comes from a deep conviction that some truth of experience cries out to be expressed, to be shown to others. So, the writer struggles to express that conviction in a work that is effective and convincing.

Paul speaks in 1 Corinthians of faith as one of three Christian virtues. He says they are faith, hope, and love, "and the greatest of these is love." No doubt the faith of a writer is accompanied by hope and love, for the writer hopes to express new insights and fresh visions of reality. The writer's work is loving work, work designed to reveal deep truth. As a writer, I believe I have something to say, that I have the talent and craft to express a certain vision or narrative of how things are. My faith is accompanied by hope that what I write will be received and understood. And this faith is driven by love, by concern for others, and most of all by fidelity to God.

More often than not, the faith of a writer is tested by failure, rejection, disappointment. "We regret to say that while your submission has merit, it does not fit with our current publishing plans. . . ." At first we cling to those pieces of paper, imagining some clue to success hidden in the formulaic language. Later, as rejection letters accumulate, we gain perspective. *It's a form letter,* we see at last. *They send these to everyone. Well, practically everyone.* Rejection is one of the real pitfalls in the writer's life. We have to grasp that we will not always be floating on a sea of adulation and praise.

Gradually, by trial and error, we learn to manage our hurt feelings, our anger, our outrage. We dust off the piece and send it out again. Or we rewrite it. Or we write something new. We buy another copy of *Writer's Digest,* join a writer's group, attend a seminar, trade ideas with other writers, develop harder shells.

Perseverance is part of the writer's fidelity. We fight to keep fresh, to avoid the pit of despond. We keep at it. We laugh things off without losing our fire.

One of the perennial questions for writers (some say it is a faith question) is whether or not to have a day job. *If I really had faith the size of a grain of mustard seed, wouldn't I quit my day job?* Even in a life of faith there is no ready-made answer to this question.

I've seen some colleagues, during my years in advertising, bloom into successful novelists, acclaimed mystery writers, award-winning short story writers. Their day jobs had supported their talent instead of destroying it. I noticed myself how the day job could heighten writing skill. Because I wrote for a living in major New York and New Orleans ad agencies, I learned how to trim, cut, polish, rewrite, accept criticism, avoid pomposity and high-toned verbiage, cultivate an ear for dialogue, get to the heart of things.

Recently, I heard Joan Didion speak about her early formation as a writer, doing photo captions for *Vogue*. She insisted that her editor's demands had helped her develop her craft.

Didion described the straitjacket of her early magazine discipline, when she wrote captions to a strict character count, yet tried to compose the dazzling phrases expected at *Vogue*. A seasoned editor would fling the copy back over her desk at the young Didion. "More action verbs!" she would demand. Didion claimed it was the making of her style.

We often perceive this day job issue as central to the writing life. If we had enough money to quit our jobs and write, shouldn't we do it? Isn't it all about courage? About faith?

Perhaps. But the money to quit your day job may not be a ticket to success. I knew one advertising woman who took a year's leave to pursue short story writing. After a year, she returned to advertising, complaining that she had not accomplished much. Apparently, the central issue was not her day job but a failure of nerve. As the year spooled on, she had been unable to refuse invitations or say no to friends intruding on her writing schedule.

She told me this sad tale over lunch. Privately, I made a diagnosis. My colleague's vision of the work itself was not strong enough to make her close the door on interruptions. I wondered (and didn't want to ask) whether *that* was a question of faith.

⌒

The writer's faith is also tested by the well-known challenge of writer's block. My worst attack came while I was working on my first book, *Turning*. I was well past the major research, and the conceptual thinking had been done, yet I could not begin. I staved off writing, worried that I was up against a "last shot," a final now or never. I could become a writer or I could miserably fail. I imagined the scorn of the critics, taunts about an advertising woman trying to write about God. "I'm afraid to write that book," I admitted to my husband.

His response was immediate. "That's pride," he said. Later, I thought his comment had been a special grace. He had punctured the balloon of my grandiosity and fear. "Be like Thomas Aquinas," he went on. "He put his life's work on the altar and called it straw."

I had completed two full-length plays and a book-length memoir. Faced with daily, even hourly deadlines on newspapers and in Madison Avenue work, I had excelled, spinning out numberless campaigns. In a three-year policy-related job, I had written testimony and full-length speeches. Why hadn't writer's block afflicted me then? Had I escaped because I was less invested in advertising work than in "my own writing"? Possibly I had assigned less value to my commercial or policy work. Even so, I knew it was all *my own writing*. Every sentence had my characteristic sound, my stamp. And, like most copywriters, I dreaded the drying up of inspiration and took precautions to avoid seizing up.

The novelist Graham Greene describes his own writing strategies in *A Sort of Life* and *Ways of Escape*. He did not begin to write until a story had fully matured. He seemed to fear the power of the beginning sentence to narrow or curtail his idea. My own tactics were more like gym workouts: stay loose, stay limber, leaf through magazines, read books on creativity (James Webb Young comes to mind), take long baths and loll about until inspiration shows up. Unless, of course, time runs out. Then write and be sure that inspiration will follow.

I suppose writer's block and stage fright are first cousins. We lick them by thinking more of others (readers and listeners) and less of ourselves. We think of the word to be given. This, too, is an exercise of faith, following the commands of love. We become more generous and less self-preoccupied.

So what are the rewards of writing? There are quite a few.

Fame is not nearly such a lure as it first seems. As it gets closer, it dwindles. That famous Andy Warhol fifteen minutes (if one ever achieves it) is gone in a quarter of an hour.

When *Turning* was published it got a favorable review in *The New York Times Book Review*. Television interviews followed. The book was praised by reviewers. I remember the day of publication, the twentieth of June. I stood in my kitchen in Queens, New York, and waited for planes to fly over releasing sworls of confetti. But the day passed uneventfully.

As the weeks passed, I saw I had gained a certain reputation, a modicum of success. Editors were asking what I planned to do next. I took pride in all of it, yet success—even the admiration from perfect strangers—seemed beside the point.

Was it all about fame? Was that what I had been dreaming of and working for? Was that where faith was leading? I didn't think so. Maybe my writer's dream was never about fame at all. Words of John Milton came to mind, denouncing fame as "the last infirmity of noble mind."

What, then, is the reward of writing? Where is the satisfaction of this calling? Partly, I sense it in the response of readers, when a note comes from a stranger who says my writing has made a difference in his life. Yes, that is consoling.

There are certain privileged moments like these. I recall meeting Father Henri Nouwen at the Image conference in California. He heard my name and recognized it. "Emilie Griffin!" he said. "Clinging!" (*Clinging* is my book on prayer, which Nouwen had read and endorsed without knowing me, ten years before.) His recognition told me that the words of praise he gave to my book were a real appreciation, not just a pro forma duty.

But these are not the only rewards of writing: the money, the praise, the connecting with readers, the critics and their occasional acclaim. In this life of writing as faith, there is still something deeper that matters.

Do I really know what it is? Or does it slip away from me, a goldfish disappearing into the dark waters of the pond? I think the deepest satisfaction comes in the writing itself. One word follows another, one sentence builds on another, ideas chase each other down the page, somewhere in midchapter the hint of a conclusion comes. Then the music starts.

Or, if it is a narrative, the ending comes into view. The last scene develops like a print in a darkroom, under fluid.

Revelations may appear in the second or third draft. No, this would be a better opening sentence! Begin here. Move this passage up. Sometimes small changes are epiphanies.

Deep in the act of writing, a seed sprouts, an egg is fertilized, the organism grows. Life, embryonic at first, takes shape, gets bigger, starts to kick, then pushes out of the womb, yelling for all its worth.

I live at the deepest level of spiritual practice when I am writing. Much later on, when I skim the published text, I am only trying to reconnect with the sweetness and anxiety of writing, the instant when something exploded from nothing into its own surprising DNA.

⌒

For me, when all is said and done, writing is an act of faith. The faith is in the wanting, the yearning, the desire. It is desire that drives us to spin and to weave—out of words, out of sentences—some fabric of meaning, a picture that clarifies, something that sheds light, makes sense out of confusion or even warms the heart. Such yearning is an aspect of faith. The will also comes into play: the will to create some new expression of reality, and the will to stay at it until it is done, and done well. That will, that fidelity, is also an exercise of faith.

I admit that Samuel Taylor Coleridge had it right in his *Biographia Literaria* when he wrote, "The willing suspension of disbelief for the moment, which constitutes poetic faith." Coleridge says we must suspend our disbelief for the literary illusion to work. But I think we writers must suspend disbelief in ourselves. Instead, we put faith in our own powers, our gifts, our call to write.

And we put faith in God. We believe in God, who has charged the universe with meaning. We are in touch with God, who asks us to proclaim the truth of things as they are. To express our faith, we dig deep for understanding. Sometimes we cry out in anger against the offenses that should not be. With Gerard Manley Hopkins, we ask, "Why do sinners prosper?" We question God, we challenge the things in creation we don't fully understand. But also we observe, we take delight, we remember, we celebrate, and we praise.

FURTHER READING

For further reading, I suggest books that support and encourage writers in their task. One that has strong overtones of faith is Annie Dillard's *The Writing Life*. A second book of encouragement is *On Becoming a Novelist* by John Gardner. Although he concentrates on fiction, the book is worthwhile for writers in all fields because it focuses on the courage and discipline of writing. Anne Tyler, in reviewing Gardner's book, called it "a marvelously detailed account of the creative process." Other books that nourish writers' confidence are first-person accounts by admirable writers on how they have approached their writing. Graham Greene's short books *A Sort of Life* and *Ways of Escape* provide real insight. Muriel Spark's memoir, *Curriculum Vitae,* gives a clear account of the writer's commitment. Reading biographies of accomplished writers is a fine way to grasp the meaning of the writer's call. One such good biography is *Jane Austen: A Life* by Claire Tomalin.

7

Entering into the Dark and Essential Places That Writing Demands
On Writer's Block

Keith Miller

Writer's block is that sudden cessation of the interior creative process as it is moving a writing project to completion. The block may be experienced as a kind of mental paralysis that keeps writers from accessing their own ideas and motivations. Creative excitement evaporates and is replaced by feelings of inadequacy, self-doubt about one's ability, and fears of failure.

The subjective experience of writer's block may be different for each writer depending partly on the primary reason each is writing. Some writers find writing to be an interesting hobby or avocation. For others, writing is just a way to make a living. And for still others, writing represents vocational, even personal, identity. A sudden unexpected blockage that turns out the lights, so that the writer can no longer proceed to the completion of a writing project, can elicit very different emotional reactions from different people, from mild irritation to fearful specters of starvation to shame about perceived failure.

Even though writers often laugh about this fickle disappearance of the muse when they get together, writer's block is not funny when it happens to us when we're alone, staring at our word processors. In this essay I will describe ways I have experienced writer's block. First, since writer's block is the interruption of a process that I go through each time I write, and since my first solution to the interruption includes the utilization of particular parts of that process, I will explain briefly how the writing process works for me.

The Writing Process

When I begin to write, my mind can become so flooded with ideas that I've had to invent a way to keep my focus—to avoid writing four or five different books in one manuscript. This difficulty has led me to adopt the following dramatic solution that not only keeps me more focused, but also injects the intimacy and passion I feel while writing *into* the manuscript without depending on a special technical knowledge or a unique skill.

In order to stay on course as I was writing my first book, in 1965, I described specific people to whom I would write this book and kept them with me in my imagination. These people represented the primary audience I hoped to reach. This in-house audience consisted of a family of four: a husband (a young business executive, about age thirty-five), his wife (a thirty-three-year-old stay-at-home mom), and two young teenagers, a boy and a girl. This family not only attended church but were active in it. They believed in God, but (if truth be told) were bored with a lot of what took place during the worship service. They had a sense that much that went on in worship and other church programs had little or nothing to do with their "real" lives (that is, making a living, taking vacations, participating in hobbies, or making love). Although they didn't talk about it, they were restless, in search of a new direction in life. I imagined that this family sat across from me at the dining room table where I was writing my book in longhand on an 8½-by-14-inch yellow pad. My goal was to offer them, through my writing, the direction they sought.

My daily writing process began with prayer each morning as I sat down to write. My imaginary audience was there, but I did not—you will be glad to know—demand that they join me in prayer. As the writing began, I filled the yellow pages, keeping in mind the specific (but imaginary) family to whom I was writing. Each day I would try to write for two or three hours. During writing time I kept focused and animated as I told my imaginary audience, via the yellow pad of paper, the insights I had discovered about the subject and how I sought to inject these insights into my day-in and day-out relationships with God and other people.

One day, as I finished writing and was reading over the new pages, I felt the urge to read my day's efforts aloud to the little family across the table. The results that came from vocalizing the text that day changed my life as a writer from that point on.

I had not realized that when I wrote I sometimes used stilted or pious-sounding language that I would never use in a real conversation with people for whom I cared. I also realized that one of my illustrations was included primarily to make me look more intelligent, but it wasn't really necessary to communicate my point. When I finished reading aloud to my little audience that first day I laughed out loud! Then I apologized for talking down to my "friends." As I made this confession, I sensed a strange feeling of intimacy with those imaginary people.

Over the past forty years, many readers of that first book, *The Taste of New Wine,* have responded, "I had the strange sensation as I read your book that you were writing to *me* particularly." When I heard that repeatedly, I knew that the intimate feelings that grew over time for my imaginary audience somehow transmitted through the pages into the personal lives of some readers.

Although the audience changed with succeeding books, this sense of intimacy I felt for each imaginary audience continued. In fact, it turned out to be a major part of the solution to the frightening and smothering experience of writer's block, when it dropped on me like a wet blanket, extinguishing all light to see the thoughts and ideas I'd gathered for the interrupted project.

What Happens Inside the Mind When Writer's Block Starts

What we call writer's block is actually one example of a frustrating universal inner experience that may only be noticed in times of stress. Before discussing particular manifestations of writer's block, let's take a look at a simple working model of the human mind and the disruptive experience that can materialize for anyone into a show-stopping silence of creativity.

Imagine that your mind is an inner cavern two-thirds full of an opaque liquid. The top third of the cavern that is not liquid is your conscious mind, in which all your thoughts, memories, and ideas are readily accessible to you. The liquid lower part is what Sigmund Freud called the "unconscious," a sort of underwater storage vault or library for filing ideas, thoughts, and experiences that remain a part of you, but are outside your conscious mind.

Another of Freud's ideas about the human mind is that a censor guards the door to this unconscious, unseen storage area of the mind. This gate-keeping censor acts like a librarian, retrieving stored information when we want it, delivering the idea, illustration, or fact that we need to our conscious mind. But the censor may also, at times, prevent us from getting into our conscious mind to retrieve facts, dates, names, illustrations, or ideas that we need to negotiate life (or complete a book).

The frustrating activities of the fickle and intractable censor in everyday life are well known to everyone, not just writers. For example, virtually all of us have had times during school examinations when we could not recall some fact that we knew very well, only to have it spontaneously materialize with great clarity in our mind after handing in the exam and walking out of the room. The censor had withheld and then released the information we wanted.

Censor blockage of familiar or well-known material can happen to a writer assembling an artistic book project. The writer may suddenly be locked out of the storage library of his or her own mind, with all of its creative material. The special word, illustration, or logical conclusion—which was clear five minutes before—suddenly cannot be accessed.

Although the magnitude of emotional reactions to this baffling and seemingly irrational lockout may vary, some combination of negative, even fearful feelings of frustration, self-doubt as a writer, inadequacy, fear, and even shame ascerbate the experience of writer's block.

Using Your Audience to Overcome the Block

Let's say that you are sailing along, writing each day and becoming aware that you may have a good book or article when you're through. You begin to fantasize about people reading it and liking what you've written. Then, with no warning, you can no longer see what was plainly before you a minute earlier, as if electricity had failed in your home at night, leaving you temporarily blind, stumbling over familiar objects you cannot see. Writer's block has arrived.

One morning I woke up and started down to the writing room, excited about the way the manuscript to my book had been flowing. But when I sat down and finished reading the last page I'd written the day before, my only thoughts were, "No one is going to want to read this—it's absolute drivel." In a few minutes, I had forgotten all about my audience and about God, only thinking, "Why in the world would I think I could write this book?" I was powerless to proceed—I felt an awful aloneness. Then, through the thicket of fears, I remembered my imaginary audience, stared in their direction, and decided I'd just tell them what was going on.

I picked up a pencil and started to write to them on a yellow pad. "You know, I'm really stuck, and I can't seem to get a foothold anywhere. And I'm really getting frustrated and insecure. I can't write today, but I remember that last night I thought I would write about . . ." And I began to recall and explain to them what had been on my mind and what I could remember from earlier jottings. After two-and-a-half pages of "conversation," I was writing the book again. It was as if the act of *explaining* what was going on inside myself to these people—the fear and frustration—broke the spell and primed the pump, restarting the flow of my writing process. When I finished writing that day, I tore up the two and a half pages of "conversation" and said a prayer of gratitude.

What Happened?

I thought about what had happened. Our imagination has an elastic quality. For instance, in the imagination, a small social slight can grow—within minutes—into a vicious rejection that threatens to ruin one's life. In the same way, a small thought can jump into your mind like a little monkey suggesting that you can't write. In five minutes, this irritating little monkey-thought expands into King Kong, paralyzing you as in a nightmare, leaving you unable to escape your negativity and self-doubt.

Now, many books later, I've learned why being alone with writer's block feels so frightening and terminal. The imagination becomes paralyzing in its power, a phantasmagoria of danger and failure. These negative inner images can expand into terrifying, widescreen, high-definition monster movies. The normal mind can be overpowered by them.

The good news I learned is that when we can reveal our exaggerated fears to another person or persons, we are bringing the inner, boundaryless, elastic "monsters" out into their actual size in the present moment. And in the shared reality of the present moment, our fearful thoughts shrink to their actual size in relation to other things around us, and we can move beyond them. (Most successful psychotherapies and spiritual guidance utilize this same insight—that verbalizing and describing fearful thoughts can normalize them.)

The "cure" I stumbled on is not dependent on having an interior audience to speak to. But taking the frightening images out of my mind and describing them on paper (even to my imaginary audience) shrank them into reality. The key factor was my reaching out to describe the smothering feelings to someone else, even though the audience was imaginary. At that time, I don't know if I would have told any real people I knew the strength of the shameful fears I experienced during writer's block.

But when I learned that bringing fearful feelings out into the open before others could prevent ungrounded fears from becoming unreasonable eschatological monsters, I realized that writer's block is just a human problem that is particularly painful for artistic people. It no longer tyrannized me, as I was able to share my honest feelings with my imaginary audience. Since that time I have learned to share the blocked experience with a "live" friend or writers' group as soon as possible. There is something about the honest confession of fear and inadequacy in real time to a specific person or persons that can often dissolve the fear around that problem, releasing the blocked information or motivating energy.

Writer's Block as a Spiritual Diagnostic Tool

Since I am a Christian whose writing is a spiritual vocation, as well as an intellectual and financial one, writer's block has come to have special spiritual meaning for me. As a serious Christian, it has been my habit to face and try to remove any behaviors, attitudes, or motives that keep me from loving God, others, and myself. Since writer's block affects my relationships with God, my audience, and my family negatively, I have come to believe the experience may well be a signal that there is something unacceptable in me that needs to be faced and changed before I can finish the particular project I've been working on. But how does a writer discover the unacceptable spiritual cause of the block?

I now believe that the cause of writer's block for each person may be shrouded by the cloud of denial in that person's life. When my own mental processes freeze or become negative, I have learned to ask myself, "What am I afraid will happen when people read this book?" Usually, this fear is something I can't see or articulate at first, but something I feel would be painful or damaging for me as a mature writer and committed Christian. My unconscious attempt to deny that fear is like trying to hide a beach ball by pushing it underwater. It takes both hands to hold the beach ball under, leaving me with no hands for the work I am eager to complete.

Some examples of "unacceptable" things—usually character defects that I have repressed—that have surfaced following episodes of writer's block are:

1. Early on I was unconsciously afraid that the book I was writing would be considered unorthodox or even unchristian by some readers whose approval I sought (such as ministers, theologians, denominational officials, or even some members of my family or friends). I had unconsciously blocked my project with writer's block to avoid facing the feared responses.

2. Another time, when using a confessional style to deal with a problem, doubt, or fear long hidden beneath the radar of the gatekeepers of conventional wisdom, I feared that my confession of having the problem would cause some readers—especially gatekeepers—to think I was mentally or emotionally impaired or immoral. In order to avoid facing such reactions, I shut down.

3. Once, writer's block occurred when I was writing about an area I had studied and examined for some time, but about which I did not feel I had the academic credentials to critique authoritatively. Since I was writing in a different *style* than the experts used, I secretly feared that they would reject the *content* of my argument as being naïve. My unconscious censor protected me by shutting down my writing process to avoid facing the charges of ignorance and naïveté.

The spiritual truth I discovered through this process of articulating my hidden fear is that *each fear* I did not want to face revealed one or more aspect of a false god in my life about which I was in denial (such as pride, wanting to be considered more than I am, and not trusting God with the outcome of my work). In each case, the cure came when I became willing to confess to God that I loved myself and, for instance, my reputation more than I loved God—and then decided to surrender my entire life and my future to God as I understood God.

As I have done this over the years, I have felt an increasing joy and freedom to risk taking chances in order to find new ways to communicate the things I want to share with readers. And now when writer's block comes, it is less frightening because I realize that I may be about to discover another fear or insecurity that keeps me from the freedom of writing—and living—for God with integrity and love.

FURTHER READING

While my approach to writing through writer's block comes through my own exploration and spiritual journey, other writers and artists have been helped by the following books, which offer differing explorations of the topic.

One book that offers a helpful guide to writing through some dark passages is by Luci Shaw. Her book *Breath for the Bones: Art, Imagination and Spirit* provides a safe place for writing through difficult places, while offering a grounded guide to the creative process.

You may also want to read Madeleine L'Engle's book *Walking on Water: Reflections on Faith and Art*—a classic text that doesn't shy away from mistake-making, patience in craft, or exploring the interior terrain.

For a writing guide that explores the roots of creative resistance see also Vinita Hampton Wright's *The Soul Tells a Story: Engaging Creativity with Spirituality in the Writing Life.*

Another resource is Dennis Palumbo's *Writing from the Inside Out: Transforming Your Psychological Blocks to Release the Writer Within.* "Stuck" creative writers may find help in *Art & Fear: Observations On the Perils (and Rewards) of Artmaking* by David Bayles and Ted Orland.

Part Two
 GENRES

8

Deeper Subjects
On Writing Creative Nonfiction

—•—

James Calvin Schaap

Dokmai, whose gleaming skin and bright eyes made her seem much younger than her sixty years, had been telling me about her job at a packing plant, where she stood each day, like so many of her Laotian-American friends, knife in hand, making a cut or two at chunks of meat moving slowly down the line. I wanted to write the story of her life.

We spoke through an interpreter, and at first, her words were guarded. But then, slowly, an hour into the interview, she came to understand that I wanted to know her story and her eyes softened behind an abiding, gentle smile. I asked some tougher questions.

I offered the idea that lots of "Americans" (that was her language, and I pointed at myself) wouldn't likely choose a job in a meat-packing plant, didn't want a job like hers. I asked her what she thought of her work.

She nodded. It was clear that she loved it.

"And why is that?" I asked.

She answered quickly, in just one sentence, and I looked at the interpreter. He shrugged his shoulders. "In Laos, she says she had to do *all* the butchering."

Immediately, the bloody carcass of a water buffalo flashed into my imagination, with Dokmai standing there alone, a machete in her fist, the jungle behind her. In Laos, she'd done all the butchering; here, in America, on the line at the packing plant, she made just one simple cut. Here, her work was a hundred times easier. That's why she loved her job.

Her answer exposed privilege—mine—in a way that left me speechless, astonished as I was at the reality of my own cultural blindness. In that single answer, Dokmai taught me more about immigration than a year of news specials.

⌒

When I consider the nature of creative nonfiction (it's awful to be defined by negation, isn't it?), that moment with Dokmai comes to mind because central to the genre is research, our gaining an understanding of someone, something, some event that's not our own personal experience. Personal narratives and memoirs use fictional techniques and are cousins to creative nonfiction, but those genres are always about the writer. Creative nonfiction is not about the writer, but about someone or something other than the writer and his or her story. Creative nonfiction requires the writer to look around, eyes wide open. It requires asking questions. It requires exploration—lots of it.

To be sure, imagination is required of creative nonfiction writers every step of the way, in what we hear and what we discover, as well as what we say and how we say it. But creative nonfiction, for me at least, always begins with people like Dokmai, with places like jungles, with details like machetes. Creative nonfiction doesn't begin in the imagination because the essence of the genre is the stories and characters and settings we writers don't know. Creative nonfiction begins outside of ourselves, begins in worlds that trip us up on the limitations and prejudices we're often blind to.

Creative nonfiction begins with an impulse to share the joy of what we've learned, somehow, from someone else, from a Dokmai, for example, whose simple answer to my question explained so very much about immigration. While the first significant characteristic of creative, or literary, nonfiction is that it offers what must be the verifiable truth, there's more.

Here's how Lee Gutkin, editor of the journal *Creative Nonfiction,* defined the genre in a recent television interview. Creative nonfiction, he said, is "a way of capturing a real subject—whether it be politics or economics or just profiling a person—but doing it in a literary way. It's a way of elevating the whole concept of nonfiction or journalism."

Gutkin's definition points specifically at a second central element of creative nonfiction: its "creative" or "literary" character. In telling the story, creative nonfiction picks up the tools a fiction writer uses— it creates characterization, for instance, and uses scenes or "beats"; it records dialogue—not only what is spoken, but how ("her eyes softened behind an abiding, gentle smile"). Frequently, creative nonfiction paints scenes with the close description one expects in a novel or short story. Creative nonfiction is not fiction, but it may use any of the tools on the fiction writer's workbench.

Perhaps the classic example of creative nonfiction is Truman Capote's much-heralded *In Cold Blood,* which is categorized nonfiction because of its reliance on the truth about the grisly murder of a rural Kansas family in 1959. However, by immersing himself in the lives of the characters—the murderers themselves—and using techniques of fiction, such as multiple voices, Capote's chilling rendition of the story offers us a book that feels far more like fiction than ordinary news journalism.

There are those—I may be among them myself—who believe that Capote went too far journalistically in his pursuit of the story. Many believe that what he wrote was, in fact, more fiction than nonfiction. Nonetheless, no single book was so important in the establishment of a genre as *In Cold Blood*. Why? Because Capote entered the story as a journalist, deeply concerned with the facts of the story; but when he wrote the book, he did it in such a way as to make the story feel much like a novel. That's creative nonfiction.

⌐⌐⌐

I have been reading a new book about the war in Iraq, *The Long Road Home* by Martha Radaatz, a wide-ranging yet vivid account of the lives of soldiers and their families, lives forever affected by an awful firefight one day in Iraq in 2004. Radaatz is a highly respected television news reporter who brought all her researching skills into unearthing the story. By profession, she's a journalist. But her concern in *The Long Road Home* is not simply the objective facts of what occurred one awful day in a place named Sadr City—who, when, where, why. Because she wants her readers to feel the horror, the grief, the reality of war, she takes the time to create scenes—the look of a desert dawn that morning in Iraq, the vacant stare of a young spouse watching the phone after hearing the news of a battle hundreds of miles away. We not only see the action, we feel it, deeply, fearfully.

Martha Radaatz's book is creative nonfiction of the highest quality, as impressive in the reach of her research—it seems she knows so much about so many of those who were affected by that firefight—as it is riveting in its telling. *The Long Road Home* offers the truth about an ambush well-reported in the national news media. But by employing the techniques of a fiction writer—creating the scene, revealing depth of character—she brings us into the story in a way that ordinary news reports never, ever could.

Her book is, first of all, about a squadron of soldiers and a battle; but when readers finish the book, they know they've discovered more. The real subject is war itself, inexpressible grief and sadness. In many ways, *The Long Road Home* is about those of us who've known sorrow and heartache—and that includes most of us.

What creative nonfiction like *The Long Road Home* shares with news journalism is the importance of investigation—of exploration before we can make any attempt at conveying the truth of what happened. What it shares with fiction, however, is a target—the human heart.

⌒

If you stumble on an abandoned farm where some local tells you a sad family story once took place, a story that still haunts the neighbors; if you are held hostage by that story and you want, like nothing else, to write it, as it happened, then you want to write creative nonfiction. But you have to want to learn that story, to discover what happened, to determine who and when and why. Creative nonfiction doesn't rely solely on imagination. It researches as promiscuously as journalism must because the stories it tells aren't just based in truth, they're told as they happened.

One of the most memorable weeks of my life was one I spent with a World War II resistance fighter from the Netherlands, a woman named Diet Eman. Until she'd consented to tell me her story, Diet had purposefully put her own incredible suffering during those years out of mind. What that week cost her emotionally could probably be measured in tears—because there were many. What I learned, not only about the history of Nazi occupation, but about starvation, about putting one's life on the line, about righteousness and sacrifice simply cannot be measured. My research began, simply enough, with listening.

When this seventy-year-old woman finally enlisted my help in writing her book, I'd thought to write it like *The Hiding Place*, a kind of novelistic interpretation of the World War II story of Corrie ten Boom, another Dutch resistance worker who had also hidden Jews from the Nazis who occupied their native Holland.

In fact, Diet Eman had known Corrie ten Boom, who had also been imprisoned in a prison and a concentration camp, and worked with her in the Netherlands after the war. Diet told me that she'd asked Corrie at one time, years later, why there were elements of *The Hiding Place* that simply weren't true, elements that had been brought into the story. Corrie had told her, once you give your book to a writer, it's not yours anymore.

Diet was quite up-front about not wanting me to alter the facts in this book about her life, a book we would eventually title *Things We Couldn't Say*. She didn't want the story to be anyone's but hers. She wanted the verifiable truth, not something graciously molded for drama.

At various points throughout the telling, I wanted to know more than she gave me, more than she remembered; I wanted badly to imagine my way into scenes that she could, or would, only outline. But I knew hers was not going to be a book "based on" the story of Diet Eman. Creative nonfiction wouldn't let me speculate, wouldn't let me imagine, wouldn't let me dream.

My job was to piece her story from all the fragments she'd given me, a sometimes rambling collection of anecdotes about the war years, and to shape it into something told in her voice, something with the rhythms and beat of narrative, with as much description as she provided, with characterization I needed to find from and within her telling. Creative nonfiction is as resolutely committed to the facts as is the very best news writing.

⌒

Yet, creative nonfiction always has a subtext. It always offers more than meets the eye, a reality behind the story. Metaphor is important in creative nonfiction because the story itself—while compelling—almost always suggests something greater, some theme or issue or idea.

When Dokmai so glibly told me that she loved her work on a factory line because making a couple of cuts on a chunk of hindquarters was a better job than carving up the entire animal, she taught me far more than I knew about the those who willingly take the jobs that many of us disdain. She taught me something about a species of blindness created by my own affluence. She helped me see and helped me understand.

What she said that night was as unforgettable as it was because her answer found a place in my heart, the place creative nonfiction writers often wish readers to enter into through their work. Creative nonfiction almost always marshals the facts in such a way as to tug us toward some truth about life and death and all those issues people talk about under the heading of "the human condition." That abandoned farm and its scattered family? Their story, in the hands of a writer of creative nonfiction, will not simply be names and dates and court records. That story will certainly be about the people who lived there; but at the same time, like all great stories, it will be about the people all of us are.

Tracy Kidder's marvelous account of the life of the medical doctor Paul Farmer, *Mountains Beyond Mountains*, is the story of a man deeply—almost madly—driven by the desire to alleviate the suffering of the poorest of the world's poor. By way of unsparing descriptions, the book, which is more than a biography, brings the reader into the hospitals, prisons, and slums Farmer frequents.

And yet, the book is about us—all of us. In showing so clearly how Farmer lives, it's impossible for readers not to measure themselves by Farmer's life, not because Farmer is a saint but because the portrait is so richly human that all of us feel our own hearts beating in the narrative. Kidder followed Farmer's world travels, but the fictional techniques he uses in the telling make his subject step off the page.

⌣⤳

If the mission of creative nonfiction is to direct the truth to the heart, then idea plays a significant role. Most creative nonfiction writers create work that may well be called "essay" because what they fashion from their material has a thesis. It may be hidden or only slightly referenced, but what drives the story being told is an idea. Phillip Gerard, in *Creative Nonfiction*, says the genre "has an apparent subject and a deeper subject." The idea—the thesis—is "the deeper subject."

Joyce Carol Oates's remarkable book *On Boxing* likely relates more about America's most violent sport than most readers even care to know. But in the process, she also opens up ideas about masculinity, about racism, about suffering and survival. There are "deeper subjects" moving hither and yon across the ring before us.

Creative nonfiction, like its close relative the personal essay, often enough has two plotlines. One of those plotlines is the story itself—in Dokmai's story, the narrative of her life in Laos, her escape to Thailand, her eventual immigration to America. That narrative would give any book about her life its most obvious architecture.

But there is also another plot, if I may call it that—another strategy of sequential action, something else unfolding throughout the narrative. This is the often dramatic revelation of the story's own theme or idea, which speaks to the questions, What does this all mean? Why am I being told all of this? The second plot is the slow revelation of "the deeper subject."

I risk oversimplification, but to put it succinctly, creative nonfiction frequently works inductively, so that, by the end of the tale or tales, readers arrive not only at denouement, but also at the point where they discover, often on their own, the theme or deeper subject of the story itself. Everything crystallizes somewhere near the end. That effect brings satisfaction and perhaps even joy to readers, and is a characteristic of creative nonfiction.

Such a strategy may be more frequent in shorter forms of the genre—in the personal essay, for example, than in book-length, literary nonfiction. But it's worth repeating that the truth-toting nature of creative nonfiction means that suspense rises not only from the action of the story, but also from the steady and sometimes puzzling manner by which the central idea itself finally forms clearly in the reader's mind.

⌣⌐

An old novelist friend of mine once told me that all stories are shaped like C's—that is, they leave a certain empty space into which the reader brings his or her own perceptions. That gap is the place where we discover truth ourselves, rather than having it revealed to us.

Stories begin somewhere, then circle around, and, like a flushed rabbit, eventually return somewhere adjacent to where they began, forming something close to a circle. Great stories are not O's; they don't complete themselves, leaving nothing to the reader's own imagination. Really fine stories leave a gap and thus require a reader's participation.

That gap is crucial and must be artfully accomplished, with at least some perception of who exactly is your audience. Today, my aged mother likes her stories fully closed, just about O's, so she doesn't have to think too much about what she's read. My literary friends like their C's stretched out nearly into I's. They don't want to be spoon fed; they much prefer a significant and larger role in interpretation. I's suggest question marks. O's end in exclamation points.

If all stories are C's, then one of the dilemmas most writers face is, when does one say too much and when does one say too little? The question is not just a matter of concern in creative nonfiction, but it's primary in that genre because most nonfiction totes a central idea or thesis. The danger of shipwreck for the closed C (the O) may be greater—more deadly.

Mind a warning here. Any storytelling that proclaims its central idea on a billboard is preaching and not singing. All good writing—even sermon writing (although I'm not a pastor)—is basically begun in exploration. The best creative nonfiction, like the best fiction, begins in questions, not answers. Always leave space for the reader's participation. How much? That's for you and your audience to determine.

⌒

And now I happen to find myself at a place where I can turn back, like a C, to where I began. Moments in time like Dokmai's prophetic answer happen to us often, not just in research, but in life. One of the joys of marching into unknown territory is the plausibility—the near inevitability—of surprise; and nothing is more important to narrative than surprise. Research—looking into the lives of other people, other places, other times—can be as full of shocking blessings as life itself.

I thank God for Dokmai's answer. I'm a wiser man for what she taught me.

Tracy Kidder claims he stumbled into the story of Paul Farmer, the story that became *Mountains Beyond Mountains*, simply by meeting the man. "My favorite teacher once used to talk about how writers often have their best stories bestowed upon them, seemingly by accident," Kidder explained in an interview. "I felt as though, in meeting Farmer, I'd been offered a rare opportunity."

How can we nurture a frame of mind and heart that allows us to be surprised? Begin by keeping yourself open, a task sometimes especially difficult for believers. I've been trying to write for a long, long time and teaching forever, it seems. But I hope and I pray that in whatever time the Lord gives me he won't stop giving me Dokmai moments that grab me by the scruff of the neck and drag me around until I understand what I've not seen before, and have the chance to write it down. I hope my life is as full of epiphanies as it was when I watched my first child grow. I hope I never stop learning.

If writers, particularly creative nonfiction writers, pursue what needs to be accomplished, all the while desiring to be brought to their knees in awe, they will find their way to good writing. There is a sweetness in being blindsided by life, by truth, by a dark corner suddenly illumined.

There is sheer joy in epiphany. If we are what we write, the first writing requirement would be to nurture a character in oneself that wows easily, that runs itself silly chasing breathlessness, that is as easily stunned as delighted. Writers need to be, in a way, worshipful.

Dokmai made me want to write her story, not simply because her pilgrimage was unusual and therefore inviting, although it was; she made me want to write her story because a single answer she gave left me speechless. That's something worth saying, worth writing about. That's something worth a story, something worth an even deeper story.

FURTHER READING

Creative nonfiction may well be the new kid on the block but its short history doesn't mean that it has no classics. In addition to those I've already mentioned, let me suggest a few more that have created a literary presence. One of my favorites is Ian Frazier's *Great Plains*, an incredible romp through this nation's hearty midsection, a book that features everything from the Indian wars to the phenomenon that was, and is, Lawrence Welk. Frazier's playful wit is exceeded only by his dogged seriousness; it's a masterful historical dance upon the broad open land he calls "fly-over country." Maya Angelou's *I Know Why the Caged Bird Sings* is a beloved contribution to the genre, as is Annie Dillard's *Pilgrim at Tinker Creek,* which holds special interest for Christian readers. And no believers should miss Kathleen Norris's *Dakota* and *Cloister Walk,* both already classics as well.

If you're interested in knowing more about the craft itself, look for *Writing Creative Nonfiction: The Literature of Reality,* by Gay Talese, a fine anthology that features some of the best writing of the genre. How do people do it? Check out *The New New Journalism: Conversations with America's Best Nonfiction Writers on Their Craft,* by Robert S. Boynton, where you will find all kinds of good advice.

9

The Novel Taking Form
On Building Fiction

—⋅—

Doris Betts

When Flannery O'Connor was asked before one of her southern audiences, "Why do you write?" she promptly answered, "Because I'm good at it." People recoiled; in our region, modesty is thought to be automatically transmitted with the X chromosome. But Miss O'Connor, a committed Catholic, was not being arrogant. She hastened to add that she took seriously the parable of the talents in Matthew 25, so if she wrote fiction because she was "good at it," that answer grew out of her conviction that every person's talent was a gift, that each of us has a responsibility to use that gift as well as we can and, by that use, return it to the Giver at least as large as ever—possibly larger, if service has helped it to increase.

Though this Presbyterian agrees with Miss O'Connor on the why of writing, we differ on the how. She wrote in "The Fiction Writer and His Country" that if a writer can assume that her audience does not share her beliefs, she may have to make her vision apparent through shock: "To the hard of hearing you shout, and for the almost-blind you draw large and startling figures." That is certainly one method, but I—like many mothers and kindergarten teachers—have found that the whisper can also be effective. There's quite a range between characters like O'Connor's startling Hazel Motes in *Wise Blood* and Ann Tyler's quiet Ian Bedloe in *Saint Maybe;* as there's a range between times when Jesus inveighed strongly against a "generation of vipers" and other times when he stooped and silently scratched words in the ground.

In O'Connor's world, the road to Damascus runs straight through south Georgia, where God's grace gets thrust almost violently into people's lives; in Walker Percy's world, some awkward pilgrim will set out, of his own free but uncertain will, on a quest to determine God's very existence. Graham Greene works with apparent moral failures like the whiskey priest of *The Power and the Glory*. C.S. Lewis extracts a whole pre-Christian novel (*Till We Have Faces*) out of 1 Corinthians 13. In Susan Ketchin's collection of writer-interviews, *The Christ-Haunted Landscape*, novelists as different as Lee Smith, Reynolds Price, Harry Crews, and Will Campbell express their talents in very different styles.

If, in O'Connor's stories, the Grandmother recognizes the Misfit and then perishes, or Mrs. Turpin gets called a warthog in two different ways, or the Holy Ghost continues, implacable, to descend from a ceiling stain, my own characters don't seem to earn such direct intervention. Like the descendants of Job's second cousins once removed, they struggle through a long weekday process that includes losses and boils until, in the end, God does not so much answer their questions as silence them, simply by being there, so that my characters end by saying—or maybe whispering—"Mine eye seeth Thee." Some of them might add, "That is You, isn't it?"

Neither a shout nor a whisper spoken by a believer who thinks she distinguishes a dim gestalt of the Holy Spirit operating in this world will convince a nonbeliever. Answered prayer is the easiest of all experiences for an atheist to explain away—until he has one answered himself. I work mostly with characters who gradually, sometimes reluctantly, become alert to the possibility that human life is more than meets the eye. Being alert to possibility is, after all, the way most writers generate stories. Metaphor, simile, symbol suggest meanings beyond the concrete objects from which they arise. The "seeds" for stories that Henry James described seem to arrive as mere coincidence.

My most recent novel, *Souls Raised from the Dead*, got underway because on my daily commute to the University of North Carolina–Chapel Hill, I came upon a chicken truck wreck beside the highway. Seventy-five hundred capons, raised in houses heated and lit by electric current—chickens that had never set foot to ground before—were loose from the overturned truck. They flew; they hobbled with bloody wings; they banged into passing windshields. Neighbors were catching some in tow sacks for lunch and dinner. Imbedded in this scene, with wounded chickens flapping past his head, a state trooper was trying to bring order out of chaos in a tableau both horrible and funny. And the look on his face? Pure existentialist despair. If Jean-Paul Sartre had lived in Chatham County, North Carolina, he would have recognized this as Page One, though perhaps we would have written different paragraphs at the end. In my case, that chicken truck wreck opens a novel in which a highway patrolman longs to protect his daughter from all harm at all times, to rear her as perfectly as if she could be kept in unnatural isolation like those chickens. But of course, there is no way to give children a perfect or a perfectly safe life. There will be wrecks in their lives, too. There will be escapes, freedom. And, in time, there will be injury.

As I was starting the novel, Harold Kushner, a Massachusetts rabbi, published his book in memory of his son who had died at age fourteen, *When Bad Things Happen to Good People*. Here he brought traditional Judaism to wrestle with the old question of undeserved suffering in a world he believes to be ruled by both a good and a powerful God. Kushner never pretended that people get what they deserve in life; he did not accept the premise that God sends pain for testing or improvement, nor that either God or ourselves are to be blamed for the cancer, the avalanche, the drive-by shooting. What he did choose to do was what my own characters must: cope with grief and loss, struggle for hope, help one another. In my novel, the survivors, not the sick child, are the "souls" that are to be raised, raised from despair.

Not until the novel was done did I notice that its structure had taken the shape of an anecdote Kushner tells, an old Chinese tale about a woman whose only son had died. In her grief, she went to the holy man and said, "What prayers, what magical incantations do you have to bring my son back to life?" Instead of sending her away or reasoning with her, the holy man said, "Fetch me a mustard seed from a home that has never known sorrow. We will use it to drive the sorrow out of your life." At once the woman set off in search of that magical mustard seed. She came first to a splendid mansion, knocked at the door, and said, "I am looking for a home that has never known sorrow. Is this such a place? It is very important to me!" They told her she had certainly come to the wrong house, and began to list all the tragic things that had befallen that family. Since she had been through misfortune of her own, the woman decided she might be the best person to help these wealthy people, so she stayed to comfort them. Later she continued her search for a home that had never known sorrow, this time going to a shack, next time to a city slum. But wherever she turned, from palace to public housing to country club, she listened to one story after another of sadness and misfortune. Ultimately, she grew so involved in ministering to other people's grief that she forgot about her quest for the magical mustard seed, never realizing that it had—in fact—driven the sorrow out of her life.

At the end of my first chapter, I could see that a young girl was going to have a life-threatening illness. In her name, Mary Grace Thompson, I managed to whisper both "Grace" and the surname of a poet named Francis, and to lift an invisible hat to a Flannery O'Connor character as well.

But what should the illness be?

A friend and rather literary doctor at the UNC Medical School, Bill Blythe, was the obvious adviser. His father, LeGette Blythe, had published many biblical novels, *Bold Galilean* being the best known. His son, a former student of mine, became an editor at *Esquire*. Could Dr. Blythe suggest some fatal illness? (Not leukemia: that's been done; and not that obscure literary ailment that kills off the girl in *Love Story*, what we usually call "Ali McGraw Disease.") Dr. Blythe suggested kidney failure because, he said, "We can cure almost everything else."

Immediately, the moment of the chicken truck wreck turned transparent and permeable; I went falling through it like Alice through the rabbit hole, into the whole territory of medical ethics—those questions our grandparents seldom raised in Sunday school. What about organ transplants, heroic deathbed measures, surrogate parents, euthanasia, abortion, genetic manipulation? I began to be homesick for O'Connor's "Greenleaf," with its unambiguous bull that would drive a horn straight into Mrs. May on the last page.

And how to tell this medical story? O'Connor's "large and startling figures" could easily be transformed into melodramatic actors on some TV "Disease of the Week" program with soaring background music and Tylenol commercials. Should it be written in cool and clinical prose? Or should I assign to the state trooper a bookish narrator-friend who reads theodicy on the side? And if the daughter died, how could the story be anything but morbid and depressing, as even the gospel story would be if it stopped short on Good Friday or Holy Saturday?

Anton Chekhov's story "Grief," which is also about a father's loss of a child, confronts all these risks of being melodramatic, sentimental, overdone. On a cold winter night in St. Petersburg, the driver of a horse-drawn cab is transporting passengers back and forth through the swirling snow, to parties and back, to the opera, the cafe; and tonight the job is very hard for him because his son has just died. All evening, he tries to tell his passengers about that death and about his grief, but they're too busy to hear. They talk with one another about the magnificent overture, about the velvet gown their hostess wore, about the quality of the evening's wine. At the end of the long, cold night the cab driver goes through the falling snow and down to the stable where he tells his grief to his horse. "Listen," he says, "suppose your colt died and you lived on? That would be sad, wouldn't it? Yes, that would be sad."

For Chekhov, what keeps that moment full of sentiment but just short of sentimentality, is its brevity and understatement played out against the snow, that whirling frigid snow that cools the moment, that holds it in tongs like a specimen. In North Carolina we lack blizzards, so I set out to balance a story about illness and death against not cold snow, but the warm counterpoint of life and laughter. One axiom of storytelling is that if a character is to die in a way that moves the reader, that character must first be made fully alive; otherwise no more emotion will be generated than when strangers' names appear in the obituaries.

But writers turn into foster parents themselves, and once I concentrated on bringing Mary Grace to life as a normal, funny adolescent, I was in the same position as her trooper father. I did not want to lose her. When Charles Dickens was publishing *The Old Curiosity Shop* in installments, it's said that when the sailing ship bearing the latest chapter came into Boston Harbor, people were waiting on the docks, shouting, "Did she die? Did Little Nell die?"

Nobody was waiting to hear hard news from me. I ran head-on into a wall that was half theodicy, half writer's block.

When, in *The Brothers Karamazov*, Ivan debates how God can be both all-good and all-powerful, considering how much the innocent suffer—especially the innocent children—he becomes enraged at injustice. He offers to give back his ticket to life because if God is good but not all-powerful, then God can't intervene against cruelty; but if God is all-powerful and simply unwilling to intervene, then how can God be good?

In *How to Read a Novel*, Caroline Gordon cautioned against the "novel of ideas." My translation is that it's better for novelists to get to metaphysics via a chicken truck wreck than the other way around. Stories, like lives, naturally give rise to questions. To start from philosophical premise risks constructing a tinker-toy novel, a paint-by-number portrait, a Barbie doll sculpture, in which all content is a means to an end and a means with the life wrung out. Students in writing classes can easily be paralyzed by the question I once heard a teacher ask: "Do you really have anything to say?" Only allegorists start from that end and work backward. Most writers set out to tell a story, knowing that who they are and what they believe will whisper its way in just as they do in daily life; their personality and beliefs will sink below the word-surface like a stain; they will be inside events the way the peach seed grows inside the peach.

Despite my first assumption that I was writing a medical novel, I saw that its pages had been whispering religious implications all along—that from the first glimpse of that chicken truck wreck, the subject matter partook of Jesus' lament over Jerusalem in Matthew 23:37 and Luke 13:34.

That's how "The Hound of Heaven" by Francis Thompson got into the plot, because I did not hold the same theological position as Rabbi Kushner. I was not even in the exact position of that Chinese lady who sought the magical mustard seed, since I knew a different mustard-seed story. Kushner's book lifted the ceiling off the Old Testament and flooded that view of God with the light of mercy and compassion, but it still wasn't the same as the New Testament.

Beyond this block of metaphysical seriousness came the psychological one of refusing to let Mary Grace die. I invented several miraculous cures, brought in European specialists. I wrote splendid sky descriptions. Many minor characters entered the book and most of them made exits.

Then Czesław Miłosz, Nobel prize–winning poet, came for one semester to the Chapel Hill campus where I teach. Awestruck, I could not think of any conversation to make with a man who had survived the Nazi occupation of Poland, had written so many memorable poems, and had called tragedy "awareness of the philosophical deep, over which—and thanks to which—science and technology have erected their flimsy palaces." But the great man proved accessible and humorous, a devout Catholic whose wife grew up in eastern North Carolina. By then I had already titled my novel *Souls Raised from the Dead*, but now stumbled across its thematic epigraph in a poem Miłosz wrote in memory of his mother who had perished in World War II.

In the poem, at Mass, after hearing the morning's Scripture, the speaker of the poem meditates on how God has not made death and does not rejoice in it. He thinks of Jesus raising the girl by saying "Talitha, cumi," a New Testament moment that makes him "rise from the dead / And repeat the hope of those who lived before me."

Discovering this poem, like the chicken truck wreck, seemed fortuitous, seemed lucky. It seemed like Grace.

All my novel had to do was to repeat that hope or, as T.S. Eliot would have said, to "redeem the time." The soul to be raised was not that of Mary Grace from death, but the soul of her father from despair—the ultimate death. And the end of the novel does not shout about heaven, does not draw large and startling pictures; it only whispers. In the end, Mary Grace Thompson does die and her father's heart is broken, but he makes a start toward hope in divine mercy. Hope may even be whispered so softly that not every reader will notice that there are fathers and Fathers in the final paragraph.

Would I describe it as a "Christian" novel? That durable noun first used to name the saints at Antioch seems to spoil to a rancid adjective with a slight whiff of the Pharisee. Between Pittsboro, where I live, and a neighboring town is a gas station with a sign: WE TITHE. BUY GAS FOR JESUS. I drive on by.

Yet, at the end of the novel, my bereaved state trooper father is entering the state George MacDonald ascribed to one of his own characters, an elderly Anglican priest named Thomas Wingfold, who has spent his entire life serving the church. Now Wingfold is old; his doubts have awakened again; he is afraid of dying. He also wonders if his life has made any real difference or had any meaning at all. Wingfold ends with a version of the Pascal wager, hoping eternal life is true, choosing it even if he can never be absolutely certain. In his diary, Wingfold writes these words:

> Even if there be no hereafter, I would live my time believing in a grand thing that ought to be true if it is not. . . . Let me hold by the better than the actual, and fall into nothingness off the same precipice with Jesus and John and Paul and a thousand more, who were lovely in their lives, and with their deaths make even the nothingness into which they have passed like the garden of the Lord.

FURTHER READING

There are many books on art and religion, literature and religion, and over the years I've benefited from nuggets found among their varied aesthetics and often conflicting advice. But among those I go back to are *What Is Art?* by Leo Tolstoy, *Religion and Art in Conflict* by Samuel Laeuchli, *Art and the Question of Being* by Hans Kung, *Time and Myth* by John S. Dunne, *The Art and Craft of Religious Writing* edited by William Zinnser, *Faith and Fiction* by Philip Stafford. (This last book discusses the fiction of Graham Greene and Francois Mauriac, but draws larger conclusions.) But because each writer works out his or her own answers to the demands of art as vocation, I've benefited most by reading the words of other writers who were working out those answers, often quite different, through their stories and poems, or sometimes speaking directly to the issue in nonfiction. That list would be too long to name here, but among them would be Walker Percy, Flannery O'Connor, Frederick Buechner, Alice McDermott, Mary Gordon, Kathleen Norris, Dorothy L. Sayers, G.K. Chesterton, Madeleine L'Engle, Ron Hansen, Luci Shaw, Reynolds Price, W.H. Auden, John Updike, Czesław Miłosz, Simone Weil, Annie Dillard, Larry Woiwode, Marilynn Robinson, T.S. Eliot, Will Campbell, Graham Greene, and many, many more.

10

Being Smarter Than We Are
On the Short Story

Erin McGraw

"The short story": the phrase introduces the challenge. A story is supposed to be *short,* and both readers and writers can be forgiven for imagining they hear a starting gun as soon as the telling begins. Part of the thrill of a story derives from its speed and deftness in negotiating tight turns. How much can these few words, taking up so little space, reveal about the world and its inhabitants? How much can they move us?

Some people, looking at this form that seems so simple, allow themselves to think that writing a short story will be easy. Only a few scenes, just a wee bit of narration. Why, a person should be able to knock one of these off in an afternoon, with time left at the end of the day for coffee.

Do not be deceived. Yes, a story should be short, as many writers have reflected, but not small or trivial. If anything, stories tend to be more filled with significance and moment than novels, because so little space is available. Stories need to get *on* with things. Even the most languorous-seeming tale is aware of its agenda, and behind its apparent laziness it is quietly building the grid of images and echoes and associations by which stories carry at least some of their meaning.

The grid is necessary because so much meaning needs to be imparted quickly. At some level—not always strictly the narrative one—the writer must develop conflict, escalate the tension surrounding that conflict, create a critical moment of breakthrough, and, typically, provide some reconfiguration. Then, too, the writer will want to create memorable characters who are clear and bold in their outlines without becoming caricatures. The action should feel arresting without being implausible, the overall movement suggestive of larger meaning without feeling either coy or ponderous. And the story should be beautiful, remembering that beauty in literature can be brusque, or violent, or funny. It's quite an agenda.

Because of the need to do so much in such a small space, story writers are often particularly aware of language. To say that the ocean is as flat as a parking lot can help to establish a becalmed day; if that simile also reflects the character's dullness of perception, or hopelessness, or obsession with cars, then it helps the character to leap into a greater perspective and take residence in our minds, exactly the kind of move that stories make over and over and over.

Stories are sometimes called "lyric narratives," because their narrative action, the pure business of storytelling, is often buttressed by a powerful lyric movement, in which meaning is suggested by association, implication, shades of meaning—allowing us to infer significance without being directly told. In this way, stories work in a fashion similar to that of lyric poems, with images working as powerfully on the imagination as scenes and action. Stories may be thought of as the halfway point between the tight, associative meaning of poetry and the comparatively loose narrative weave of novels.

Dwelling in that halfway point, stories are a specific and unique form, hewing to their own rules. Unlike poems, stories typically give concrete form to a whole world, equipping it with teakettles and asphalt and the neighbor's irritating cat. And unlike novels, stories seek not to illustrate a whole, lived existence, but to generate a compressed understanding of some aspect of that existence, relying on patterns of image and symbol as much as plot, dialogue, and exposition. The forms are fundamentally different, but the aim is pretty much the same: to give voice to our existence. It is a tall order.

"Oh, come on," a person might understandably—if stubbornly—say. "A novel takes years to write, and usually requires research and many different kinds of expertise. Surely writing a story is easier than that. To write a story you only need to know a few facts, and then fill in the rest with images, right? Child's play."

The best answer to that understandable, stubborn person is to tell her to go ahead and write a story, then study the result. Most of the time, for most of us, the early efforts are dismaying. What we've written is short, all right, but it misses the essential spark that makes a story memorable. The quality that makes a story throb with life and significance is missing, and in its place is a short string of words. The missing element is a certain kind of vision, and that vision is not simple to attain.

Novels can be compared to landscapes illuminated by a mild afternoon sun. A viewer has the leisure to contemplate the display, to ponder shadows and light, to study the overall effect. Stories, on the other hand, are like landscapes illuminated at night by lightning—what we catch is only a glimpse, and may be exaggerated, but what we manage to see is dazzling and sears itself into our vision.

This is not to say that every story must be sizzlingly dramatic. But successful stories—I cannot think of a single exception, from the quietly compassionate tales of Anton Chekhov to the gaudy, supernatural comedy of Flannery O'Connor—find their way to a revelation of experience. Because of the shortness of the form, that revelation controls every word choice, image, and action. Lacking the novel's easygoing breadth, stories gain instead a kind of chiseled, focused energy that feels like urgency. This *must* be said, the story implicitly cries. It *must* be heard. Small wonder that many story readers put down their books or magazines at the end of even a very short story, needing to take a breath and recover. If the story writer has done his or her work fully, the ending will resonate in a reader long out of proportion to the duration of the reading.

Now, let us be honest. All of us have read stories, many of them, that have not left us with this sense of resonant completion. The world is well stocked with stories of laudable ambition but regrettable achievement, stories that we readers can almost see straining for importance and profundity and effect. We can hear the grinding of the storywriter's bones, smell the sweat. Unfortunately, we can see and hear all that work more clearly than we can see or hear the fictional world that is supposed to be moving us to tears or laughter or some other emotion. Perhaps you have written such stories. I have.

The strictness of the story's requirements and its unwillingness to give comfortable harbor to any kind of excess of plot or style can leave a writer with the literary equivalent of stage fright. In our eagerness to achieve a story's elegant, decisive movement, we strain, pummeling the language, giving our characters odd, sometimes baseless actions (or alternatively, actions so generic as to induce narcolepsy in the reader), or otherwise doing harm to what seems to be such a simple and unremarkable and easy activity, just telling a story, for Pete's sake.

Let us not fool ourselves. There is nothing easy about telling a story.

A story is a full exercise of art, by which I mean artfulness. Although the classical short story impresses readers with its apparent naturalness, in fact every line and motion is contrived. Art makes what is contrived appear natural, even inevitable. So, in Chekhov's "The Kiss," it is a necessary contrivance for the army officer Ryabovich to enter a darkened room by accident, so that he might be kissed by the unknown lady who has mistaken him for another officer. And it is a further necessary contrivance for Chekhov to make us understand that Ryabovich is aimless enough and fuddled enough to lose his way when wandering through his host's enormous house that he might very well stumble into the room where the soft, fragrant arms are ready to clasp him. And so forth. Every detail must be put into place, ready to perform its necessary narrative action when called upon.

In the end, does the darkness impressed upon Ryabovich by that flirtatious kiss intended for another man, that contrivance, have resonance out of proportion with the duration of the telling? Oh, yes. We come to see not only how circumscribed is Ryabovich's life, but the startling heights to which his hopes soar when he receives that unexpected kiss, bestowed like grace. Suddenly his world is filled with possibility—not because he has earned such possibility, but because he exists, and because life is, at every turn and moment, plump with what might occur.

So much the sadder, then, when he acknowledges that he was nothing more than the recipient of an accident, and that the kiss meant nothing whatever. His life, no smaller than it ever was, now seems cruelly circumscribed because, for a moment, he perceived a greater potential. But who could wish never to hope? Is life worth having, if hope is so treacherous a companion?

Chekhov says none of this. But even the most careless reader will come away from "The Kiss" obscurely moved, filled with complicated emotions that resist easy explication. It is as insufficient to say "The Kiss" is about a kiss as it is to say that it is about the futility of hope; neither statement begins to do service to the richness of this small masterpiece.

Here, precisely, in this conjunction of action and its suggested significance, is the place where short stories often find their greatest expression. The interesting action, that which can be told, is made still more interesting by its foundation upon the images and metaphors that help to express the full quality of a life. If Ryabovich were to ponder, on his way back from the party, "I used to think that I was an insignificant mouse of a man, but now, by this mysterious, romantic moment, I understand my place in the universe to be grander than I had ever dreamed," the reader would quickly—and rightly—wince and put down the story. If Ryabovich instead looks at a distant gleam, unable to make out whether it is a bonfire or a light in a window, and fancies "that the light looked and winked at him, as though it knew about the kiss," we swiftly understand not only his welling joy, but also his inchoate sense that the entire universe, right down to lights in the distance, understands his joy and shares it with him. Even Ryabovich is not quite so besotted that he would risk spelling out this sweet thought in so many words, but he doesn't need to. The image carries his hopes for him.

Images and metaphors often work in this way, expressing figuratively what would in plain language be clumsy, stepped upon. Such use of language is what is meant by the often-repeated advice to story writers to "show, don't tell." Language that shows a situation invites readers into a piece of fiction in a special way, bypassing the intellectual/cognitive pathways of comprehension. Instead, images and metaphors encourage us to enter a work imaginatively, putting ourselves in Ryabovich's place as he happily ponders the light shining in the direction from which he has just come, or later in his bunk, feeling his kissed mouth tingle as if he has been eating peppermint drops. The more we feel the sensuous details of Ryabovich's life as if they were our own, the more readily we will feel his emotional life as well. And the more we share his emotional life, the larger our own experience becomes, for we have lived a life as real, for a moment, as our own. In this way, both the making and the reading of fiction are profoundly moral acts, since fiction requires that we enter a world with all the intelligence and courage at our command.

Like most moral acts, writing fiction is also often humbling. For one thing, so often, especially in early drafts, our writing is so bad! We sit at the desk, filled with a powerful sense of compassion and oneness with our character, pouring out page after page expressing the character's deepest yearnings. We return to the desk the next day and see, dismayed, how clumsy are the effects we achieved, and how sadly obvious the details that had seemed revelatory when we wrote them down. Perhaps we are not the unalloyed geniuses we had thought ourselves, forging, like James Joyce, in the smithy of our souls the uncreated conscience of our race.

Sighing, we get to work, replacing this adjective with a better one, thinking through that moment and arriving at a fresher action or perception, junking this entire scene because, frankly, it stinks, and there's no point in trying to save it. Thus, inch by inch and word by word, do we take the bald clay of our first imaginative engagement and refine it, thinking and rethinking our way into our material until it becomes subtler, more complicated, and, I would argue, fundamentally more truthful.

While the path to that rethinking very often comes by way of tinkering with language, its most obvious effect generally concerns character. Stories may take shape around a particular action—the mistakenly bestowed embrace in "The Kiss," a literally fatal gesture of outreach in Flannery O'Connor's "A Good Man Is Hard to Find"— but our understanding of that action is rooted in our understanding of the person making or receiving it.

In a novel, characterization is often a fairly leisurely affair. When an action is taken, such as a parvenu buying a mansion near the water, quite a lot of time and pages might pass before readers learn that the parvenu's name is Jay Gatsby, and there is a complex reason for his acquisition. With its emphasis on compression and symbols, the short story collapses that capacity for leisure. We need to cut to the chase. Who are these people? Why are they doing such strange things? The heightened quality of a story often makes even ordinary actions seem a little peculiar, and the truly strange ones become luminous.

The storywriter's first tool for characterization might seem surprising for a partially lyric form, but it is essential: plain, workaday, capable exposition. A few straightforward sentences that set out a few facts about the character's situation can save writers—and readers—a world of difficulty. Once readers know a few fundamentals important to the particular story, such as the character's age or job or family situation, they are free to move toward interpretation and, more beautifully, experience. We see this in the opening of "The Kiss," which right out of the gate lets us know that all the battalions of the N Brigade have been invited to the general's house, and that Ryabovich, with his slumped shoulders and spectacles, is uneasy at the prospect. Once these facts of situation and personality are in place, Chekhov is free to let us see the world through Ryabovich's nearsighted eyes.

And then? And then we can experience the world as Ryabovich does. Once we see with his eyes, or those of any character, we can share his feelings—in a small but important way, we briefly *become* him. Equipped with Ryabovich's timidity, readers can feel his tumultuous joy, followed by his sorrow. Comprehending the radical terror felt by the Grandmother in "A Good Man Is Hard To Find," we find ourselves understanding her strange actions—even if we don't want to. O'Connor, in her brilliance, gives us more than we would ask for ourselves.

At least, this is how fiction works when it is written well, with full honor given both to the craft and to the characterizations being put on the page. We are called on to know our characters better than they know themselves, and perhaps better than we know ourselves. When they behave badly—and almost all stories, fictional or not, are generated by somebody behaving badly—our task is not to judge them, but to comprehend them, and then to allow our readers to do the same. It is not easy.

To write in this scrupulously nonjudgmental fashion can go against our grain. If we're writing about a character whose behavior we find repugnant, it feels meet and right to point out the character's moral poverty. It feels immoral *not* to do so. But to do so is almost always to write bad stories. We are called to know our character specifically, and to bring her onto the page as clearly as we can. Art calls on us to see the world as she does. Art calls on us to pull on her values and perceptions. Art calls on us to put aside everything we think we know and enter the world unarmed, trusting only art to keep us safe. If the activity feels grossly foolhardy, you're doing it right.

To work in this way can be, to say the least, profoundly uncomfortable and, far from seeming moral, can feel utterly immoral. Can it be right to set aside the values we hold as precious? We are so rarely given the opportunity in life to hold forth to an audience. Shouldn't we seize the opportunity when it comes our way to point out that racism, snobbery, and SUVs are bad?

No. For one thing, few readers are apt to disagree that certain values, painted broadly across an unnuanced canvas, are deplorable. In that case, the writer is doing nothing but presenting an opportunity for reader and writer to smugly agree on their moral delightfulness, and as pleasant as this activity is, it is not art. In fact, stories of this sort are sermons wearing sheep's clothing, and while sermons are good and necessary things, they are best left in the hands of professionals. No less a moralist than Flannery O'Connor remarked that when she wanted a sermon, she'd go to church. And she did.

There is a more insidious way for sermons to sneak into fiction, and that is by way of the explanation. Yes, our character is a terrible bigot, the explanatory way will tell us, but we should not hold it against her. Her bigotry is not her fault, because she grew up in a racist time/grew up in a racist family/grew up in a racist place. She is doing the best she can, coos the explanation. Really, we should feel sorry for her. There now. Isn't that better?

By my lights, that is worse. Not only does such an approach degrade the character, it degrades the reader too, supposing that our acquaintance with human nature is so slight that we will accept that a complicated human reaction can be reduced to a simple explanation. Beware of explanations in fiction, especially short fiction, where you generally do not have room to return to a point.

Good fiction exists as an exploration, not an explanation. In the most satisfying stories, we are brought into the mind of a character to explore the reaches of his or her experience, and to imaginatively sample for ourselves how it would be to live such a life. Once we set aside pronouncements and begin to see our own fictional world at the level of experience, we might see details, correlations, or ideas that we would never have seen before. They will not always be beautiful, though sometimes they will be. Sometimes we might scare the willies out of ourselves. But we will begin to perceive a richer and more complicated world than we have seen before, which is one of the gifts art gives to the artist.

Does that mean that everything we know is wrong? No. It means that everything we know is often irrelevant, and what we "know" may well get in the way of what our work is trying to show us, if only we'll look.

The business of writing a story—trying out words, trying out ideas, writing characters or scenes or motifs in and then out again—is in itself an exploration, with plenty of wrong turns along the way. We may think we know our story before we start writing, but stories have a way of changing under our hands, and the idea that had seemed so glittering and delightful when we started can start to seem silly, or dull, or may just plain run out of steam on page 8. Instead, we start thinking in another direction. Maybe our character, lovesick and bankrupt, wouldn't join a circus, but would do something else—rob a bank, join a church, run for president. Suddenly, our story veers into a field we hadn't foreseen, and the next thing we know, we're writing a story we'd never meant to write. This is not a bad thing. In general, it is a good thing.

Our generating idea—the notion that got us fired up to write in the first place—is rarely bad, but it's rarely good, either. It's as much as we can see of character and situation from the outside, but as we climb inside our material, we start to see more and in greater depth.

We begin to understand more about what drives our character, and what he is capable of. In short, we see the qualities that can only be appreciated with deep acquaintance, and we are then able to bring the new understanding to our readers. So, if we find ourselves writing a story quite different from the one we'd set out to write, that's often a reason to celebrate, even if we don't feel all that celebratory. "But this isn't the story I meant to write!" dismayed writers sometimes say. No, it isn't. It's better.

Writing a story that keeps changing, a story whose direction we may not be sure of and whose ending is unclear, can be an unnerving activity. In particular, finding a satisfying end to a story that has felt more and more out of our control can be mystifying and frustrating. Okay, so our main character is now a baker instead of a CEO, and fine, what was supposed to be a story about a deep-sea exploration is now about the marriage of a son in a distant state, but what does this all add up to? We can tell that some kind of story is taking shape, and parts of what we've done seem pretty good, but what does it mean? Trying to find the ending can feel like trying to see a distant goalpost through thick fog—we squint and sidle and blink, trying to see what we cannot see.

The metaphor feels apt because it is precise. We are trying to see what we cannot see. Endings of stories are rewritten more than any other section, as writers try and try and try again to find the moment that brings a story to a new level. The stakes here are higher than at any other point. We want to give the readers a sense of surprise, yes, but not shock. The ending should reveal something that had not been seen before, but once on the page, feels consistent with everything leading up to it. To do this, what is required from the writer is nothing less than our fullest intelligence—fuller than whatever preconceptions we brought to the work, fuller than perhaps we've ever called on before. Stories expect us to be smarter than we are. We need to see what we could not see until, as we furiously squint and rewrite and squint and rewrite, we finally find our way to something that we had not see before, and that is beautiful in the truest sense of stories—full, wise, and satisfying.

And we are changed as well. Tired and exhilarated, we have been shown by our own words that the world is different from what we thought, and that our first thoughts—which had seemed so fine!—were only the beginning of a long road. It is an exceptional lesson that every story proffers. It is the business of art, always.

FURTHER READING

The world of short fiction is so wide that there is hardly a wrong place to start. *The Atlantic Monthly* editor C. Michael Curtis has edited two surprising and rich anthologies, *God: Stories* and *Faith: Stories*. They are filled with funny, dark, cranky, sublime stories about characters in search of transcendence.

No writer in the twentieth century wrote stories more fiercely or directly about faith than Flannery O'Connor. Her *Collected Stories* should be on every writer's shelf. Right next to that volume should stand *The Collected Stories of Bernard Malamud*, an unjustly neglected master. His story "Idiots First" is one of the triumphs of the form.

An odd and highly useful resource is Constantin Stanislavski's famous workbook for actors, *An Actor Prepares*. His exercises designed for actors are just as helpful for writers trying to learn how to inhabit a character's mind and body. They're often helpful stretches after too long spent at the keyboard, too.

11

Narrating Our Lives
On Memoir

Virginia Stem Owens

"How was school today?" Isn't that the first question most parents ask their children when they walk in the door? "How was work today?" we ask a spouse or friend, and, unless we're very tired, we want someone to ask us a similar question. Why? Say you go on a trip—an Alaskan cruise or a visit to a previously estranged relative. If you return and no one asks you to tell them about it, don't you feel that the experience was somehow incomplete? If no one listens to the tale of our travels or trials, we feel a little, sometimes a lot, frustrated. The human race seems to have a deep-seated need to *narrate* our lives to one another. Why?

We have an inborn need to give a shape to our lives instead of experiencing life as only a jumble of sensations—one darn thing after another, a string of unrelated occurrences. We try to give shape by identifying ups and downs, what was good and what was bad, about our day or trip or lifetime. We want to figure out what caused certain actions. Did we get fired because we were incompetent or because the boss was paranoid? Was the high score on the history test a result of hard study or pure luck?

And as we shape our story, we shape ourselves. We come to know, or at least think we know, ourselves. We all live inside some story. We have to. What, we want to know, does it all mean? And somehow we have settled on stories as the best tool with which to make meaning of our lives.

Memoirs Ancient and Modern

From the most ancient evidence we have about human culture, we know that people have been telling stories and preserving them even before they had written language. Egyptian hieroglyphics are picture books showing the exploits of kings. Cave paintings in Europe from thousands of year ago probably record how a tribe's hunt went. *Gilgamesh*, the oldest written narrative so far discovered, tells the story of the king and his friend Enkidu. By far the largest part of both the Hebrew and Christian scriptures are narratives of heroes and villains, human tragedies and divine rescues.

Any number of venues today encourage us to "tell our story." Support groups, 12-step programs, therapists, retreat leaders, even media forums such as Oprah and public radio's StoryCorps project ask participants to divulge, if not their entire autobiographies, at least the parts relevant to its current audience.

As listeners we seem to have developed an almost insatiable hunger for "true stories," or what book marketers classify as nonfiction. Witness also the upsurge in the past few years of so-called reality TV shows. And since the arrival of lipstick-size video cameras that can be strapped to one's forehead, some people have begun streaming their daily lives on the Internet. Stranger still, even more people log on to watch these unedited everyday lives. I'm taking it for granted that, since you are reading this, you are interested in reading and perhaps even writing the more shapely form of memoir than the streaming of digital dailiness provides.

Some Parameters and Pressure Points

Here are the basic parameters. Memoir is autobiographical, but not necessarily autobiography, a genre that generally spans the writer's lifetime. Usually, a memoir focuses on a slice of time in the writer's life. Elie Wiesel's *Night* records the period he and his father spent in a concentration camp during World War II. Anne Lamott's *Operating Instructions* covers her first year of motherhood. In *Down and Out in Paris and London,* George Orwell recounts his experience living among the poor of those two world capitals.

Occasionally, a memoirist captures events in someone else's life, usually someone close who has had a significant impact on the writer's own life. For instance, I wrote a memoir of my grandfather's last years, something he would not have been able or cared to do himself. However, as his life affected his eight children and many grandchildren, of whom I was the eldest, I felt compelled to gather his material in a way that explored its meaning for three generations.

Memoirists have some advantage over writers of other genres. Novelists and poets have to spend time considering what they want to write. Their material has to be invented and decided upon. But the matter of memoir is simply *there*. It has already happened and, in most cases, it weighs upon the writer's consciousness with so much pressure that, like toothpaste in a tube, it gets squeezed out eventually. For example, in *Caring for Mother: A Daughter's Long Goodbye*, I wrote about my mother's decline into disease and dementia. At first, I kept a journal in order to preserve my own sanity during that time. Later, the journal helped me organize my memories as I sought to fit the experience into my moral and spiritual universe. Elie Wiesel used memoir to make sense of the horrors of the concentration camp. In *Walden,* Thoreau worked to tie the natural world to human endeavor. So significant, so pressing were these preoccupations that they had to be dealt with in order for the writers to go on with life. We speak of recounting a tale or story; the verb recount is instructive. We are trying to make it all add up.

Thus, the writer takes what weighs on her or him (or as some would put it, what the Lord has laid on their hearts) and squeezes the material to move it from the inside to the outside where others may regard it, reflect upon it, and perhaps find a connecting thread to their own experience. Maybe it throws a little light on their path. At the very least, they know they are not alone. Others have been this way too.

My first observation to pass on to prospective memoirists came from a talk I heard Elie Wiesel give. He said, "Only write if you have to. And only write what only you can write." I take that to mean: the matter you write about should be elemental, understanding it essential to your sanity or at least your understanding of life. Writing is too hard to waste the effort on anything less fundamental.

Don't be surprised to find that what you squeeze out of your tubular self lacks adequate substance for shaping into a compelling narrative. You are writing about your own life or that of someone close to you, so that makes you the expert, right? It's not always that simple. The very leakiness of life, the way it pools and runs into other lives and events, makes it impossible to isolate from other influences. Only inside the tube can we sustain the illusion of autonomous experience. Your life began long before you were born. The strands of DNA stretch back a long way. And those strands have been kneaded and coiled and strung out by other forces ever since your birth. Discovering what those forces are and writing about them with all the accuracy you are capable of makes up much of the fun of memoir writing. What made your parents choose the place where they planted you on the planet? Finances, family connections, a thirst for adventure, their particular vocation, war? Answering these questions may take some digging, during which these archetypal figures in your life may turn into fascinating characters, whether the evidence supports seeing them as heroes or villains or just people trying to do the best they knew how.

Researching Yourself?

What large social forces have been at work in your life, pushing or pulling you this way or that? What events form the context of your life? You must remember that younger readers will not have the same reference points you do. If, say, the civil rights movement became a pivot for the direction your life took, readers under forty will need a detailed and dramatic entry into that time to appreciate its impact on you. A generic reference will not do.

When Mariane Pearl wrote *A Mighty Heart,* the memoir of her husband Daniel Pearl's capture and murder by terrorists in Pakistan, she turned what could have been a sob story into a powerful tale of triumph by giving us a richly textured account that included descriptions of the various ethnic groups that inhabit that country, its geography, various religious sects that threaten to tear it apart, the fascinating struggle between the military, the police, the national secret intelligence personnel, and the pervasive corruption infecting the government. All this was necessary to her vocation as a "truth warrior," as she calls herself and her husband. What could easily have turned into a standard melodrama, dwelling primarily on her suffering and loss, deepened to give us more understanding of the incredibly complex forces that have affected all our lives since September 11, 2001. While Mariane Pearl waited for news of her husband, she researched possible kidnappers on the Internet, clipped newspaper stories, interviewed sheiks and mullahs, filled a wall with schematic links between possible suspects, made detailed timelines to help the military intelligence officer in charge of the search. When she left Pakistan, she took with her *sixty* notebooks filled with information collected during those terrible weeks. They provided the detailed information necessary to make her story compelling.

Journals are essential to a memoirist. How you organize your journals depends on your personal proclivities. Some writers keep separate notebooks for interviews, book or Internet research, and their own initial musings. Some use note cards or physical notebooks. Some keep all their notes on their computer. Whatever method you use, keep some version of it by your bedside. You may wake up in the middle of the night with a memory that needs snaring. Trust me, if you don't pin the thought to paper at that moment, it will have fled by morning. Memory is about the most elusive of all human gifts. I have also found that misty period when one is first coming to consciousness in the morning the moment when I sometimes receive my best insights into my material. Revelation often happens when our rational minds are muddled. That's when the cap can come off the toothpaste.

Assessing Your Audience

Now we come to a delicate point. A glob of toothpaste has, by itself, little appeal. It is one thing—and often a very important thing—to write in your journal. It can be therapeutic and sometimes revelatory. But if you are writing in hope that others will be interested in and perhaps even edified by what you have to say, you must take heed of those hoped-for readers, people who don't know you and have their own lives to attend to. Their attention is at a premium. Bombarded as we are by demands on our consciousness—commercials, music, billboards, memos, e-mail, junk mail—getting someone to sit down and read a book requires craft and deliberation.

First, consider a distracted audience. Then, ponder how you might capture their attention. How do you operate as an audience for the books you choose? Are you drawn to cookbooks, mysteries, biblical scholarship? Each of those categories is geared to a different audience. Because I am blind, I avidly search out memoirs written by other blind people—this is not a large population, admittedly, but a devoted one. I also scavenge for memoirs by novelists I like. Currently, I'm reading the very funny account by Agatha Christie about accompanying her archaeologist husband on one of his expeditions to Syria. This year I found a wonderful little book, *Am I Old Yet?* by a woman who confronted her pathological fear of aging by visiting regularly an old lady in a nursing home. I chose it because I'm no spring chicken myself and also because I cared for my own mother in her declining years.

None of these books would appeal to everyone. But each connects to an audience who shares their concerns. Make a list of categories of people who would have a genuine interest in your story. Mothers of small children? Recovering addicts? Winners of lottery jackpots?

As you write with readers in mind, you will have to split yourself in two. You will be the one telling the story, but from time to time, you will have to switch into audience mode, surveying your work critically. Are you able to sustain your own interest in the narrative? Can you find a clear path through the events or do they become muddled and confusing? What's missing: perhaps a clear connection between ideas, a lack of specific illustration. Every few pages, it's a good idea to stop and read aloud what you have written. The ear can hear things that the eye will miss.

The Elusive Voice

This brings us to another essential aspect of memoir: voice. In particular, yours. Your story consists not simply of the information you want to convey or the way you organize it to produce the emotional effect you are aiming for. The best memoirs come to the reader saturated in an oral medium. Voice is an element harder to pin down than organization or facts. Voice brings the writer palpably into his or her own story. It makes sure the story enters the reader's mind and heart through the ear as well as the eye. The narrator is not merely writing but speaking, even whispering, to the reader. The distance between them shrinks to no more than a few feet.

So how is the writer to project herself over not only physical but psychic or cultural distances that separate her from her audience? First of all, by *not* doing what will keep the reader at a distance. Too many writers, either beginning ones or those used to writing in another mode, adopt a position across the desk from their reader. They want to sound intelligent, prepared, in control of the interchange. Or worse, they stand behind a podium on a slightly elevated dais, looking out at the audience whose faces they can't quite make out in the darkened auditorium. Writing in one's own voice demands (unless you are a pompous ass and don't mind sounding like one) that you come down from the platform or move around from the barrier of the desk and sit down beside your reader, who doesn't want to hear a sermon or listen to a lesson.

The reader wants to know what it was like inside your skin as you lived your story. When you had that car wreck, you were not thinking in clear, schoolteacher accents. When you raised your right hand and took the oath of citizenship, your voice tightened and maybe broke. Lived experience cannot be conveyed by trying to sound like a news anchor or your sixth-grade teacher.

It's easy enough to say, "Just be yourself. Speak in your own natural voice." But which voice? We all speak differently in diverse situations. We speak to family members in a tone and with a vocabulary that we tend to spiff up when we speak to employers, doctors, and prospective customers. Every relationship seems to require a slightly modulated tone and diction. In writing to strangers, we tend to be reserved or even shy. I wrote a letter this week to someone I don't know who might want to buy some land from me. I wanted to provide the necessary information and sound like a competent businessperson. The voice was respectful but impersonal. Then I wrote an e-mail message to my granddaughter, congratulating her for doing well in a cross-country race. The e-mail message had whoops and exclamation points and the private made-up words families develop over the years. It was personal and full of enthusiasm.

Please do not get the idea that finding a voice means simply reproducing spoken language, however. If that were all that was needed, you'd only have to switch on a tape recorder and start talking. In fact, you might try that sometime just to see how hopeless such a method would be. Spoken language tends to be a meandering river, full of sluggish hesitations and rushing, often incomprehensible, babbling.

It's wonderful to tell a story face-to-face with a friend who knows your references, empathizes with your point of view, and can break in to have you clarify a point or straighten out the sequence of your thoughts. Chances are, though, a stranger's eyes would begin to glaze over the written version of such speech after a few minutes.

This is where art comes into the craft of writing. Your job is to make your written voice sustain the immediacy of a spoken voice, while at the same time maintaining the shapeliness of your narrative. Language that conveys your attitude and feelings experienced when you were living the story must be balanced with reflective language that keeps your story within the bounds of clarity and controls the shape of your narrative. Augustine's *Confessions* reflects at length on his experiences from childhood (including infancy) through his conversion and commitment to a monastic life. But he uses the device of speaking his thoughts directly to his audience—God—in order to convey the passion he feels about God's grace in his life. On the other end of the spectrum, Agatha Christie in her Syrian memoir keeps mainly to narrative, maintaining a comic voice throughout, poking fun at the indigenous sheiks and workers and the French officials as well as the culturally clueless British crew. Who knew a mystery writer could be so funny? Yet she never slips into the harsh or cynical voice today's contemporary humorists bank on. By placing herself on the margin of the action, an observer rather than a main participant, she keeps her view wide-angle and her voice sympathetic.

Discovering your proper voice and sustaining it is no easy juggling act. It will require experimentation, detached assessment, and no doubt multiple revisions. Again, reading your drafts aloud to yourself or others can be a great help. You will be able to detect any whining, sermonizing, or other undesirable tone creeping into your story. Nothing is so self-revelatory as writing, I have found.

Authenticity

As you can see, you must be exceedingly committed to chronicling this piece of your life to work this hard. Thus, you must treat your narrative with the utmost authenticity, never forgetting that your life is a gift to be honored with your best effort. This requires excruciating honesty, although if that word makes you squirm, you can substitute accuracy. It is one of the maxims of writing that all writing is fiction. This is not only true but unavoidable. Even when you struggle to be as accurate as you can, as just as possible to the characters who inhabit your story, any individual's knowledge of reality is inevitably partial. As St. Paul repeatedly points out, "We know in part." Which does not mean there is no true and solid reality. Reality does not continually morph, amoebalike, to suit our line of sight. But, we are like the blind people in the oft-repeated story of their attempt to describe an elephant, who know only what they have experienced, however accurate each is determined to be. One feels the tail, another the trunk, a third the large flapping ears. Writers must simply and humbly accept the limitation of our own perspective as they try to bear witness to the truth.

This brings us to one of the stickiest problems afflicting the memoirist. It haunts you before you start writing and it will continue to hover over your shoulder as you are in the process. And it will linger long after your missive has been sent out into the world. It is just this: How *much* truth? Where do you draw the line? I find the question easier to answer when it concerns only myself. Not that I strip my soul bare in my books, revealing my deepest darkest secrets. Those are reserved for God. But I do try to record what is relevant to the story with sometimes painful honesty. Painful, I hope, only to me and not to my reader.

But little of what you write will concern only yourself. Your story contains other people too. Some of those are close enough to you that you worry about exposing them to criticism or ridicule. But to tell your story honestly might require describing them in less than a flattering light. What you see as merely an endearing if eccentric quirk of character they may see as an entirely admirable trait or even nonexistent. There are all sorts of ways to offend people who figure in your story, and I have probably perpetrated most of them. My long-suffering mother once requested, "When you write your next book, will you please make it about a subject other than our family?"

"But I changed the names," I protested. She merely raised an eyebrow and shook her head.

Sometimes the difficulty runs deeper yet. You may face the prospect of divulging secrets other people have worked hard to conceal. I have no absolute guidelines to provide you in this matter, only my own choices and experiences. At times I have known that what I wrote would not go down well with the person I felt was essential to my story. On the other hand, I never wrote with the *intention* of hurting that person. I just told the truth as I knew it.

Like most families, mine contains alcoholics, adulterers, and abusers. I don't drag in unpleasant details unless they are relevant to relationships or events necessary to the story. But when they are key, I don't leave them out. If you find yourself smartening up or smoothing over the truth, you need to rethink your position. Never write anything where truth is not honored. If you find that making your story public would cause more pain than you are willing to accept, write it for yourself and God.

Finally, respect the gift of memory that is such a large component of our humanity. Respect also the gift of writing that has made it possible to convey memories of other times and peoples over millennia and cultures. Through those twin gifts—memory and writing—we join our stories to theirs, enlarging and stretching our understanding of what it means to be human even to those that will follow us.

FURTHER READING

Am I Old Yet? by Leah Komaiko. A memoir of confronting a pathological fear of aging by visiting regularly an old lady in a nursing home.

The Bookseller of Kabul by Asne Seierstad (translated from the Norwegian). A memoir of a Norwegian journalist who lived with the bookseller's family for several months in the spring of 2002 and was given free rein to write about their private lives.

Caring for Mother: A Daughter's Long Goodbye by Virginia Stem Owens. An account of seven years spent as a caregiver to her mother, who was suffering from Parkinson's and dementia.

Come Tell Me How You Live by Agatha Christie. Describes how she accompanied her archaeologist husband on several of his expeditions to Syria.

Down and Out in Paris and London by George Orwell. Covers the year the author spent living with the poor as one of them in these two world capitals.

In Their Hearts by Mary Margaret Britton-Yearwood. A memoir of an autistic chaplain, about her work with Alzheimer's patients.

A Mighty Heart by Marianne Pearl. Recounts the weeks the author spent trying to find her journalist husband who was captured and then beheaded by terrorists in Pakistan.

Night by Elie Wiesel. An account of the author's experience in a Nazi concentration camp as a child.

Operating Instructions by Anne Lamott. An account, both hilarious and serious, of the author's first year of motherhood.

Prison Diary by Jeffrey Archer. An account of the British politician's first twenty-one days spent in a high security prison.

Slave by Mende Nazer. A memoir of a black Sudanese Muslim girl captured at age twelve by Arab raiders and sold as a slave to a family in Khartoum, where she worked nonstop for eight years.

Walden by Henry David Thoreau. An account of the year Thoreau spent living in a shack he built by Walden Pond, full of contemplation on nature and overloaded human life.

The Year of Magical Thinking by Joan Didion. A memoir of the author's life during the year following her husband's sudden death.

12

Steep and Exhilarating Mountains of Playwriting
On Drama

Jeanne Murray Walker

Fall. It's raining—more than a syllable of water, I can tell you—as I drive through the rolling hills of western New Jersey toward the theater where my fifth play, *The Tillie Project,* will open. The actors have already learned their lines. They're already blocking with costumes and props. Tomorrow is the final tech rehearsal. The day after, we will put on previews for the critics. Nevertheless, seven pages of script changes fan out on the passenger's side of my car. In rehearsal yesterday I understood that to be clear, the play needs more information. But when will the actors have time to learn these new lines? Listening to the windshield wipers and vaguely noticing that the trees are glorious red, I think up strategies to persuade the director that script changes are essential.

And then I think, *Who I am to ask these actors to learn new lines? What do I know about facing an audience with dialogue I've been handed the day before?* I'm not the one who has to appear on stage. I'm a poet, one of those people Shakespeare grouped with madmen—reticent by temperament, secluded by habit. Poets spend long hours with the pen or at the word processor. Poets are jewelers of language, obsessed, driven to make every word right. Permanent. But in the theater a poet can't be solitary, and *permanent* is not what you sign up for when you write a play.

The fact is, with each passing moment I'm losing control of *The Tillie Project*. By the time the play opens, it will have passed from paper into the realm of theater. Shortly after, it will disappear. A few weeks after its run, the crew will strike the set. When the screech of the last crowbar dies around two in the morning, the piece will be gone forever. I will be left with the residue, a script. Yes, it may be used as the blueprint for another production, but maybe no director will want to produce it again. I realize more poignantly every time I write a play, these are the problems with collaborating and performance.

Why Write for the Theater?

Under the circumstances, why would anyone want to write for the theater? Maybe because some of the funniest and most generous people I know are actors. Maybe because so many directors are so smart. Because what other form can fashion an audience into a community in front of your eyes? Because what other labor turns an irascible bunch of artists into a family in three weeks? Making theater together is, in some ways, like praying together. You make fools of yourself in front of one another often enough and you learn how dependent you are on one another. You start not minding it. You see it as grace.

Writing Action

It's London. The West End. I sit waiting for the lights to come up in the theater. I am spoiling for a good fight driven by a protagonist who aches with a need so powerful he has to fill it. When Romeo sees Juliet, he abandons his love, Rosalind, and goes after Juliet. Not only will he kill to possess Juliet, he will follow her into death. When Antigone discovers her dead brother's body hasn't been buried, she marches straight to the king and demands Polyneices' burial so he can rest. That's the kind of play I want, with a protagonist who acts so decisively she knocks everyone else in the play off balance. And give me an antagonist with the chutzpah to resist her. Let's see who wins.

Every character I can think of—boldfaced or conniving, funny or desperate—can be forced to change because of a protagonist's hunger. It's amazing, when I think of it. The outcome—the play's conclusion— literally grows out of the protagonist's need. You could say that the end of a play is a foregone conclusion. Oh, sure, sometimes the protagonist's action causes unintended consequences. For example, while ransacking Thebes to find out who murdered the former king, Oedipus stumbles onto the fact that he killed his father and married his mother. The protagonist in tonight's play might get what he fights for, or he might be blindsided by a force he can't overcome, but twenty-five hundred years of theater argue that if it's a good play, it will be made of action.

Making Choices

Action. It sounds easy enough. But suppose you're the playwright. The question is, *what* action, exactly? What will you give the protagonist to do? The answer depends on the protagonist's "character."

Let's say I walk into my eighteen-year-old son's room, and after years of helter-skelter chaos and lectures from me, his bed is made, his desk is clean, and he is vacuuming the floor. *This is the conclusion of a comic play!* I think, crazy with happiness bordering on hysteria. What made him do it? A gust of sanity blew through the open window of his mind. Or was it divine intervention?

If it's a play, neither. This ending is just the last domino falling. It's pushed by all the dominos that fell before it. It's the conclusion of a story, the last of a series of events and choices. What was the first domino? What was the chain of events that led to this happy outcome? Suppose I decided to write a play dramatizing the struggle we have had over his neatness, responsibility, indeed, moral character? What would I include?

I'd try to strip away everything the last weeks before his final insight and choice, because I think of plays (unlike other forms, such as a novel, where accidents are amiably tolerated) as rigorously controlled lab experiments about choice. The trouble is, I don't know what made my son change his mind. I doubt that he knows himself.

So if I were writing about it, I'd have to improvise. I would start with his character and design branching alternative choices, which would probably include some of what actually happened to him, as well as fictional events leading to the Great Insight. I would try to make the choices seem probable for a curly-haired teenager who designs websites and listens to Bach.

Character and action are two axes on the same graph, is one way of putting it. But it's not that easy. While I'm writing a play, this interconnection of character and action often seems as murky to me as the dark corner of my office where a spider lurks and weaves her webs. I try to invent a character who seems real, a character I can love, one with a problem I can care about, one who cares passionately about something, one who is a hard case, one who is odd or unique, one whose problem can be solved. Then I write a storyboard. That is, I try to imagine what this character will do. I jot actions on three-by-five-inch cards. Each card gets a specific action. Together, the cards form a sequence. There are a lot of cards. They make a kind of story.

Still, these storyboards are never detailed enough, maybe because it is almost impossible to catch in an outline the cascade of a character's choices, the complicated motives and the branching, possible consequences. Eventually, I give up and begin to write the play. And that's when I find myself quarreling with the characters.

The Characters Write the Playwright

Like other playwrights, I frequently have the eerie feeling that my characters are making choices on their own. Take, for example, Josephine, the daughter of a state senator, who is desperate to get out of her hometown, Parkers Prairie, Minnesota, population four hundred, so she can become an actress on the East Coast. It is 1904, and women are supposed to marry and bear children. She has no car, and it's generally assumed to be foolhardy for a woman to travel alone anyway. Josephine can't even imagine leaving. How will she get out of town?

To answer that question, I invent a character named Marlow. Marlow is eaten up by hatred for his father's murderer, whom he has discovered and followed from Georgia to Parkers Prairie. He builds a lean-to by the Parkers Prairie garbage dump and loiters there, hoping to find enough information to identify the murderer, who is living quietly in town. Marlow is determined to avenge his father. As soon as Josephine hears Marlow is in town, she guesses that he possesses facts she needs—how to get to New York, what to do when she gets there. Marlow and Josephine need each other. They have to get together to achieve what they want. So far, so good.

How will they connect? They can't fall into one another's arms at the beginning or there won't be any play. Agreeable characters are like agreeable people, I suppose: boring. They certainly make terrible plays. What a good play needs is characters who want something and resist one another, who won't give in and who won't give up.

It occurs to me that Josephine, because she is the daughter of a state senator, would be a bit spoiled and insolent and condescending, while Marlow would be rendered inarticulate by his festering secret and his fury. His fury needs to fascinate her, which means she must be somewhat naïve. And he can't seem to the audience like an unredeemable psychopath.

Ah ha. I'm beginning to get it. The next morning at 8:30 I begin writing. I draft fifteen pages of dialogue. I think I have a reasonably clear feel for the two characters, but the further I get, the more I realize Josephine is actually quite terrified of Marlow. She knows she needs him if she's going to get out of town, but she can't think of any way to approach the silent, brooding vagrant. What's wrong with her? He's threatening, but if she uses the right strategy, I know she can get him to talk. Why doesn't she just open her mouth?

I hadn't realized that Josephine would be so timid. I don't remember making her that way. She seems to take on a life of her own. Her refusal to speak up brings the writing of the play to a halt. I reread. There it is on paper, the beautiful woman cringing, toadying before the dark Heathcliff of the play. I am at a loss to see Josephine any other way than fainthearted. She and her choices seem like all one thing, inextricable, wound like a tight ball of string with a smooth surface. It feels as if Josephine is writing the play, as if, in fact, she is writing me.

Revision. Another Stab.

Apparently, Josephine cannot engage the Marlow I have created. I don't mean physically; I mean so they can make an emotional journey, so they can get insight and understand something about their own lives. Maybe it's the character of Marlow that isn't working in the first act. If he isn't right, Josephine may never be brought to the point of changing—that is, unless I can find another antagonist besides Marlow. Or perhaps alter Josephine's nature.

Everything is once more up for grabs. I am wild with the possibility of choices. I turn off the computer and go out to fill the bird feeder. When I come back in, I feel some bedrock under my shoes. I love Marlow's story and I decide I will change almost anything before I change that. I decide to make Josephine more self-confident, more edgy, less easily cowed. She will attack Marlow.

After working on the script for a week, I realize this Josephine doesn't work either. Marlow's had a lot of practice deflecting attacks, and he's not about to open up to someone who attacks him. It's not enough for Josephine to be a stronger character. She also needs sensitivity to read Marlow, who must be inscrutable not only because he's in pain, but because he's planning a murder. And she needs an imagination to figure out an approach he hasn't seen before. Or maybe, I worry, I have made a Marlow who can just never respond to anyone—to any kind of Josephine I can imagine. Maybe he is too deeply bitter.

But I know Marlow needs information about the man who murdered his father. To get it, he can use Josephine. She can connect him to the town. Josephine will be a weak link, because she isn't fond of people in the town herself. But that very perspective will make it easier for Marlow to connect with her. They share irony about the human race. That's a start. Then there's the possibility of love between them, explosive and strange. In order to imagine either Marlow or Josephine gaining insight and changing their lives, I need to define them, so they will engage one another.

Other Ways of Going Wrong

As I tell you this, I realize it sounds less messy than writing a play really is. The number of things that can go wrong in this simple equation of character and action is mind-boggling. For example, sometimes I've defined the character improperly for the circumstances of the play. In the first draft of the play, I may have a character who's fine for a while, but who in the end just can't plausibly get any insight. Or one who can get insight but can't plausibly act on it. Or one who can't plausibly change as much as he would have to in order to resolve the action. Or one who just isn't interested in the circumstances of the plot.

Another big mistake is to make the choices in the play out of my own preferences rather than out of the bundle of traits I have invented for the character. This may seem to be a silly error, but after all, fictional characters emerge out of the imaginations of playwrights. The two are actually not separate until the work is finished.

And then there's the awful moment when I realize that a play may not be deeply moving because the characters haven't suffered. Even in comedy, characters have to suffer to learn. We know that suffering brings knowledge. The genius of Christianity is that it recognizes the inevitability of paradox and suffering in the human predicament. But like many playwrights, I want to spare my characters pain.

Why? They're only characters.

Or maybe not. When Kafka remarked that art is like an ax that can chop through the frozen seas within us, he surely must have been speaking of the writer, as well as the audience. For me, to write a play involves an emotional journey, not merely an intellectual and aesthetic one. I hear their voices. I have to love the characters, live in their choices, suffer with them. While I am writing them, they are both me and not me.

How can I explain it? For me, writing a play is like getting into a car and looking through the windshield as if I were seeing from the character's perspective. It's not seeing a *windshield* but seeing *through* it to the road and the deer that is leaping across, flinging itself under the wheels. It is braking and steering for the characters, feeling their fear, measuring their chances, turning their wheels.

No wonder I don't want my characters to suffer. In order to invent them, I have to live their emotions. Like most other people, if I can, I want to avoid suffering.

The Foregone Conclusion

George Kaufmann, one of the geniuses of the twentieth-century stage, was persuaded to see a new play by one of his friends. At intermission the friend bubbled, "It's everything I told you it would be, isn't it?" Kaufmann replied, "Anyone can write a first act."

This story, whether true or not, has achieved mythical status because Kaufmann's quip conveys both how important and how difficult it is to write the conclusion of a play. Imagining the last scene of my play, I realize I will either have to go back and change the nature of Josephine or think up a new ending. This might be what it means to find out what you know by writing it. Or rather, by thinking ahead and *not* writing it. Let me tell you, there are some days when I am just starting a script that I go back to the beginning a dozen times to redefine a character.

The myth goes that the last act is the most difficult to write. Why? That's where characters have to get insight. That's where all the threads have to be tied up. If it seems difficult to control characters in the first, relatively easy-to-write scene, for example, how on earth do you represent the complex process of a person getting insight and deciding to change at the end? The answer? You do it by setting up for it in the first act. I think that's why, in truth, first acts are just as difficult to write as second acts. For me they are often harder. But it's the second act that lets you know whether the first worked.

I tell my playwriting students, you can't have a payoff if you don't have a setup. That's a way of saying that if there's something wrong with the last few scenes of your play, you might have to take a hammer and saw to the beginning. You might have to redefine the protagonist because the end of a play has to be contained in the beginning.

It Happens in the Theater

A script is not a play. A play is what happens in the theater. A script is a recipe for a play. It's approximately as helpful for me to read a script as it is to read a recipe book. Even though it's fun to imagine coq au vin, there's no protein in it. In fact, the only way to be sure of the relationship between a script and what happens in the theater is to both read and see the piece. Going back and forth between the page and the stage is a terrific way to improve stage smarts, which is of about the same importance for a playwright as street smarts is for a city dweller.

When I started writing for the theater, I began seeing a lot of plays. I still try to see all kinds—comedies, tragedies, satires, romances, who-done-its, political plays, old plays, new plays. Some theaters felt to me like a second home. I got to know the people who worked there and volunteered what time I could. It wasn't hard to get the crews to show me around. To walk around on the stage, where the action of my play might take place, was, for me, a good way to figure out how long a character's walk-on line needed to be, for example, and to think about blocking. I learned from play readings and talk backs by playwrights. I sat in on rehearsals every time I got a chance.

Practically Speaking

Don't write an epic. I found out about cast size restriction when the director of my second play recommended combining two of my characters into one. He didn't want an actor who delivered two dozen lines sitting around his theater, drinking his coffee, and earning equity wages. Equity wages don't seem that high if you're an actor, but they can make the difference between whether a theater makes or loses money during a run. A surprising number of theaters are one production away from closing. No wonder directors will produce new plays only if they're cost effective. They want to stay in business.

Most contemporary plays run two hours or less, take place on a limited number of sets, and are restricted to a cast of six, so I try to avoid ranging across generations and continents. Of course, a director can always design minimal sets. There are exceptions. But there's no exception to the fact that every additional set or character makes a play more expensive. This is a limitation novelists don't have. But directors worry about it, and directors control which scripts play in their theaters.

Raise the stakes. Audiences will go a long way to watch high-stakes action. Of course, therein lies a problem. Theater can seem like a video game where the point is the fight rather than the deep and complex issues the fight is about. Plays that last examine the ethical consequences of action. They are thought experiments. *Terminator* might work in the movies, but audiences in the theater crave significance.

Keep the audience guessing. In the theater, anything boring or predictable won't work because the audience catches on quickly. In other words, there is a practical pay-off for telling the truth in all its complexity and surprise. If the audience can predict what's going to happen, why should they bother to stay for the crisis and resolution? Mr. and Mrs. Schapoznikoff will get up, go home, pay the babysitter, and catch up on e-mail.

Write characters who are smarter than the audience. As one director confided in me, the reason we love Hamlet is that he's smart enough to have written the play he's in.

If This Advice Fails

If the idea I've got for a play doesn't pass some of these practical tests, what then? Especially if I feel an urgent, passionate need to write for the *theater,* as opposed to, say, write a novel? When I first started, I wrote the thing for the theater anyway. I put seventeen characters in my first play. I'm sure someone must have told me not to, but in my immense need to tell the story, I blundered ahead, reasoning that because I felt so strongly about it, this must be the one exception to the ironclad rule of small casts.

Incidentally, that play has other problems. It contains flashbacks, too, and the main character talks directly to the audience. In spite of all that, it worked, sort of. It won a major competition and has been produced nine times. But suppose I'd figured out how to combine some of the characters and leave out the narrator. Just imagine what that play could have been.

Or maybe there was never any other way to write the story. I'll never know. What I know is that, like a toddler who goes too near the fireplace, I learned from making mistakes. I will not write another play with a cast of seventeen. I don't mean to say that you can't. I am just phoning ahead about dangers that lie in the steep and exhilarating mountains of playwriting.

The Last Word

How does the story end? I write a dozen drafts of the Josephine and Marlow story. It takes several years. Eventually, I figure out a plausible way for Josephine to thread a path to Marlow's affection. The final Josephine still has a chip on her shoulder and she's become garrulous in order to overcome Marlow's silence. But she's also vulnerable. He notices her. He begins to reveal what he needs. She responds. The two help one another on their terrible and surprising journeys, and eventually they discover those journeys have been in many ways the same passage. I name the play *Rowing into Light on Lake Adley.*

There is a lot more to tell about writing for the theater—formatting, dialogue, setting, foreshadowing—and I am tempted to try, like Polonius, to talk about it all. It is enough to say that, despite the formal challenges, the bad wages, and the scarcity of production opportunities, the theater is magnificent. Actors and directors and crew have welcomed me into their sacred space with great kindness, and they will welcome you, too.

Being among theater people reminds me of visiting the hardware store in Parkers Prairie, Minnesota, in winter. Neighbors stamp snow off their boots and call out, "Hello," and shout one another's names and rib each other and argue and pull off gloves and warm hands by the heater. Each of us came for a reason—to pick up two-inch finishing nails or a cat carrier or plastic window sheeting—but high jinks and a gossipy holiday spirit take over. We realize, at some level, that our houses and our cats and our church and the hardware store itself are all part of one thing. Together we make a neighborhood. That's what it feels like, working in the theater.

FURTHER READING

If you want to write for the theater, nothing is as important as seeing plays, and it helps immeasurably to study the scripts of the plays you see. To find scripts, check out Samuel French (www.doollee.com/Publishers/french-plays.html), Dramatic Publishing (www.dramaticpublishing.com), and The Dramatists Play Service (www.dramatists.com).

For scripts by women, who are minimally represented by other presses, check Alexander Street Press (www.alexanderstreetpress.com/products/nadr.htm).

For nuts and bolts books about writing for the theater, it's worth looking at *The Art of Dramatic Writing* by Lajos Egri, *The Playwright's Process* by Buzz McLaughlin, *Playwriting from Formula to Form* by William Missouri Downs and Lou Anne Wright, and *The Dramatist's Toolkit* by Jeffrey Sweet.

A number of other books have helped me explore beyond the essentials. Among them are *Backwards and Forwards: A Technical Manual for Reading Plays* by David Ball, *Audition: Everything an Actor Needs to Know* by Michael Shurtleff, *Playwriting: The Structure of Action* by Sam Smiley, and *Improvisation for the Theater* by Viola Spolin.

If you want to submit plays to competitions and/or theaters for production, or if you're looking for an agent, consult the latest version of *The Dramatists Sourcebook*, which is published every other year.

13

A Troubled and Troubling Mirror
On Poetry

Scott Cairns

The Journey to Poetry

You're going to need a pencil.

And a stack of legal pads.

You'll want to have some company. Solitary as it often seems, the discipline of poetry offers us a way out of our private isolations, our culturally encouraged solipsism; it is a journey that joins us to an amazing community of like-minded folk, the poets who precede us.

I'm talking about both the living and the ostensibly dead. We'll come back to this mystery in a bit, but I would start by suggesting that you'll want to keep these friends at your side—or walking just ahead of you—as you find your way to poetry.

And you'll have to learn to read them in such a way that you imagine you're in actual conversation with them. If all goes well, this will become an *ongoing* conversation. They will speak to you through their poems, and you will respond to their provocative utterances in at least a couple ways: in what you make *of* them as you read them, and in what you make *with* them as you write your own, responsive poems—which will serve as your side of the conversation.

As I say, we'll come back to this mystery in a bit.

For now, I want to share a few preliminary lessons that I've come upon. You may not like them. That's really all right. You don't have to like them.

I have an increasingly strong sense that along the slow road to poetry the toughest lesson happens also to be the first lesson. My experience with young writers at various levels of their development has made it clear that if any of us fails to grasp this first essential bit, he can rest fairly well assured that his slim offerings—however earnestly he has labored over them, however sincerely she intends them—will never quite attain to the condition of poetry, and that writer will never manage to make what can rightly be called a poem.

More likely, the writer will instead continue to eke out some odd species of verse-affecting anecdote, or verse-affecting opinion piece, or verse-affecting homage to his or her commonplace experiences and familiar sentiments.

So, let's get to that first lesson: In the initial stages of making a poem, the writer must understand that poems are not about the poet, her ideas, her feelings, her opinions, or her complaints. They are not about his keenly corrective insights into the failings of his culture, his country, or his parents. Poems are, instead, about language, and about how language—when we learn to trust it—is able to operate as a way of knowing.

Given that poets—in the very midst of their making a poem—have a habit of *finding their way* to what they're thinking, genuine poems are not likely to be about anything the poet already knew—or thought she knew—beforehand.

Therefore, in the midst of the poem's initial composition, it will be helpful to the poet's progress if the poem is not thought to be a box or a bucket with which he totes his stuff about, nor as a dump truck for delivering that stuff to someone else.

Most importantly: What a poem is finally *about* cannot be understood to have preceded the actual making of the poem. A poem's primary meaning must be discovered, must *come to be* in the midst of composition. Similarly, the poem's subsequent, multiple, suggestive range of import must be understood to evolve through repeated readings and receptions in collaboration with an engaged reader. All of this is to say that a genuine poem is something of a gum whose sugars do not abate; when we come across a real poem, we are thereby encouraged to keep chewing.

Confused? Well, that's not really such a bad thing.

Between you and me, I think it's a very good start. The best.

Lesson two: if you don't genuinely love words, if you don't find quiet pleasure and uncanny satisfaction in laboring over and savoring words *themselves,* you probably should try your hand at something else. Leave the making of poems to those curious and increasingly rare folk who are happiest when poring over words, looking them up in the dictionary, speaking them aloud, feeling their textures, their percussions, savoring their flavors on the tongue, and—this is the key—pressing them for glimpses of association, flashes of revelation.

That is to say, if you think of words in a poem simply as descriptions, as fingers pointing back to prior ideas, or as memorials to a personal past, you won't be making any poems anytime soon. Hard as it is for some folks to accept, real art is, for the artist, far less referential than it is generative.

If you insist on thinking of poems as documents of your most fascinating thoughts or as evidence of your sensitivity, find another hobby. And—not to put too fine a point on it—you should step aside, get out of the way. Stop littering.

A Uniquely Word-Attending Art

If you're still reading this essay, maybe you already suppose that poetry is of a peculiar order of language—a *unique* order, even—and you may already suspect that a poem is less a document of past experience than it is a scene in which new experience is occasioned firsthand, a scene in which ongoing discovery may be expected to occur in the future. That's a very good disposition to hold on to. This may work out for you after all.

A poem, then, is best understood as a *place;* it is a scene in which meaning comes into being, where meaning is made and where it may be remade, without conclusion. Poetry is least understood when it is thought to be a public posting of private experience, of personal meaning conclusively arrived at in the recent past, and documented in retrospect.

I don't think I can shout this loudly enough: *on the contrary,* if it is nothing else, poetry is always a matter of *pro*spect.

Actual poets and actual readers of poetry know this. They know, for instance, that the surest indication of a good or great poem is that it can be read again, that it can be visited repeatedly to surprising advantage. It is safe to say that any bit of verse or prose that cannot reward our returned visits with a glimpse of something new is not a poetic bit, not rightly called a poem at all.

A real poem cannot be exhausted by a paraphrase, or even by a set of paraphrases.

One curious phenomenon to note (which may lead us to supplementary lesson 2b): I've met a lot of wannabe poets who—it turns out—don't actually read much poetry at all. They may presume to write it, but haven't much of a taste for it. The common complaint in the popular culture would have it that poets far outnumber readers of poetry. I'd argue the opposite. Readers of poetry *are* relatively few, but the actual poets are acutely fewer. The veritable multitude who self-identify as writers of poetry are simply mistaken. But don't tell them; they seem happy. Let's just choose other models, read other books.

This reminds me of a story that the poet Richard Howard likes to tell about the poet Elizabeth Bishop. According to Mr. Howard, as Ms. Bishop was concluding a public reading on a famous New

England campus she was cornered by an earnest fan—roughly her contemporary—who announced, "I absolutely *love* poetry," to which Ms. Bishop, brightening, replied, "Wonderful! Please *say* some."

So, on to lesson three.

A Clarification of Terms

More times than I can count, I have heard folks who should know better speak as if there were a self-evident distinction between "poetry" and "prose." This is puzzling. It is a little careless. And it is deeply misleading.

Given that poetry is a *genre* (one of four, as it turns out) and that prose is a *mode* (one of only two), such a commonplace distinction—poetry versus prose—manifests at least an ignorance of terms. Each of the four primary literary genres—fiction, drama, essay, and poetry—operates under its own range of conventions. Generally speaking, fiction is understood to be concerned primarily with the art of narration, drama is understood to be concerned primarily with the art of performed human action and interaction, and essay is understood to be concerned primarily with the art of argument. Poetry—the originating pulse of literary undertaking—is understood to be concerned primarily with the art of language itself; poems, therefore, draw attention to words themselves, words *as such*.

Success in the genres of fiction, drama, and essay lies in the relative *transparency* of the language employed to serve the story, the action, or the argument. That is to say, in these three genres the words on the page operate as transparencies to *move through;* in these three genres the text becomes the window to another event—a story, an action, an argument.

When we're talking poetry, however, success lies primarily in the *opacity* of the language, the ability of the words to draw attention to their own cobbled densities, and to invite the reader to encounter his or her own reflection in their surfaces. And, that is to say, in a poem, language operates, in part, as a troubled and troubling mirror. This is the phenomenon of the poetic. And while this phenomenon—the poetic—may occur, intermittently, in any of the four genres, it is the mainstay and essential purpose of poetry.

Say you're reading a novel; you know it's reasonably well written if you forget you are reading at all, if you imagine, say, that you are observing characters performing their story in the context of a scene. If, however, in the midst of such reading, you suddenly *do* begin to notice the words themselves—if, that is, you come across a particular passage whose language draws attention to itself—you might, if you were asked about it later, surmise that the passage in question struck you as a particularly "poetic" passage.

You would be correct.

Whenever literary language (in any genre) sacrifices a measure of transparency to attain a measure of opacity, we witness in that moment an occasion of the poetic.

And this is why I say that while such occasions *may* occur in fiction, in essay, in drama, they *must* occur in poetry. I would add that this quality of language is also the most reliable indicator of what we mean when we call something literary. The degree to which a fiction, an essay, a drama obtains the poetic is also the degree to which it is literary. While a popular novel depends upon what happens; a literary novel depends also on the character-revealing textures of how the story is told.

So much for genre; what about this business of *modes*? It is true enough that because most of what we call poetry occurs in verse, we may find these terms to be interchangeable. This only muddies the waters.

Simply put, a line of text is verse if it *turns* (*turn* being the very heart of *verse*'s etymology) before being forced to do so by the right-hand margin of the page; by the same token, it is prose if no such intentional turn occurs. Simple as that.

Without question, most poems occur in verse, most fictions and essays occur in prose, and whereas older dramas have tended to favor verse, most contemporary dramas exhibit a penchant for prose. That said, it is important to insist that any of the genres can occur in either of the modes.

Most of Shakespeare's plays are composed in verse; most of Edward Albee's plays occur in prose. Novels most often occur in prose, but I have read a number written in iambic pentameter or some other verse form. Essays often are shaped so that their arguments run the entire width of the page, but I have read a number of ancient essays in verse. Also, a great many contemporary texts—posing as poems—are more correctly understood to be verse essays, verse anecdotes, verse declarations, verse gripes. Moreover, we have marvelous prose poems in abundance, and we should bear in mind that anyone insisting that "the prose poem in an oxymoron" is almost certainly an ox, and quite possibly a moron—not that we need mention these observations to him directly.

Verse, therefore, is not a reliable indicator of poetic text, nor is prose a reliable indicator that a text is not a poem. The only reliable indicator of poetry is an abundance of the poetic—that experience of the words drawing attention to themselves, drawing attention to their several provocative associations, and by so doing, inviting the reader to collaborate in meaning making. That's what poems do, and that's why we like them so much. Being unfinished, bearing inexhaustible potential, they remind us of ourselves.

A Sacramental Analogy

Lately, whenever I think about the particulars of poetic language, I am drawn to what strikes me as the most suggestive of analogies— that of sacramental agency.

Throughout Christendom, both historically and at present, the church's central sacramental rite, Communion, has been—and continues to be—variously apprehended by those who celebrate it as well as by those who do not. And while I am fairly certain that this rite is never to be actually understood, I might offer two examples of how it is discussed, trusting that by these examples we might better apprehend the character of the poetic.

When I was a kid, we spoke of the matter of Communion rather simply: we characterized the event as a solemn meal shared; we also emphasized its primarily retrospective activity. My own understanding of our Communion service was roughly this: once a month, we shared grape juice, which reminded us of Christ's shed blood, and we chewed and swallowed tiny squares of hard cracker, which reminded us of Christ's broken body.

Though both actions served as powerful signs directing the mind to a very great Mystery, neither the juice nor the cracker was, of itself, mysterious. These days, most alleged poems I come across in a given week seem to work that way too. Their words point to an event, or to a stilled moment, or to a sentiment, which, mysterious as *it* may have been, remains an occasion distinct from the "poem" and its language. In most cases, then, the poem serves as the cracker, prepared so that in receiving it we might be directed to another, more real event, an event whose import and whose agency are always, necessarily, fixed in the past.

The poetic, however, is something else: it is an occasion of immediate and observed—which is to say, present—presence; it is an occasion of ongoing and generative agency. And this is a condition suggestive of Eucharistic Communion. The wine becomes the mystical blood of Jesus Christ and the bread becomes his mystical body. We might be satisfied to say that the elements *symbolize* those realities, if only we could recover that word's ancient sense of mutual participation, if only our word *symbol* hadn't diminished over the centuries into being just another word for "sign."

At any rate, as we partake of those Mysteries, we are in the *present* presence of Very God of Very God dipped into our mouths on a spoon, and we partake, incrementally, in his entire and indivisible being. Moreover, we are by that agency changed, made more like him, bearing—as we now do—his creative and re-creative energies in our sanctified persons.

This is appalling, and it serves to exemplify what I would call the poetic: the presence and activity of inexhaustible, indeterminate enormity apprehended in a discreet space. You might want to underline that.

Whether a literary work occurs in prose or verse, whether it is also characterized as fiction, as nonfiction, or as drama, whether or not it may also support additional, extra-textual narratives or propositions, it is *poetic* to the extent that it occasions further generation—to the extent, in other words, that it bears fruit.

Why, Then, the Image?

Virtually all that I have said above regarding the poetic can be manifested by our studying a well-constructed image. The reception of most poems of the twentieth and twenty-first centuries depends upon a reader's ability to appreciate what we are pleased to call the image; it is the common coin of the expansive realm that is modern poetry. Most modern and contemporary poems rely on the efficacy of their imagery for their mediating appeal; they need their words to implicate other, sensually apprehensible things, and to suggest a range of likenesses without simply being replaced by them. The image, then, is occasioned by a word or phrase producing the illusion of seeing, tasting, feeling, and the like; to a greater or a lesser degree, it is a linguistic gesture whose current and currency run ever outward in troubled and troubling implication.

As images go, the image of God merits special attention, especially for those who would see in the outcomes of our poetic production some power that is—albeit in miniature—analogous to the mystery of a thing bearing much more than is reducible to paraphrase. Just as the human person is rightly understood to be the visible occasion partaking of (but neither exhausting nor eclipsing) the invisible enormity of the God in whose Image he is shaped, so too the imagery of a likely poem partakes of a greater scope of giddy implication. Don't take my word for it; have a look at Ezra Pound's quintessential Imagist poem, "In a Station of the Metro," and see how this works.

Joining the Conversation and the Journey

So, there you sit, poised above the pristine paper, prepared to engage the matter on the page as genuine and living discourse, hoping to participate in the long conversation and the ongoing communion that is literary tradition. Here's what I suggest: find some likely collaborators among the poets who have come before you, and keep them by your side as you proceed. Gather a sympathetic circle of these friends to accompany you—and to instruct you—as you make your way.

My own circle includes, but is not restricted to, such trustworthy mentors as Samuel Taylor Coleridge, Emily Dickinson, Constantine Cavafy, Robert Frost, Wallace Stevens, W.H. Auden, and Elizabeth Bishop. And my longstanding habit of writing includes having at least one of these mentors by my side as I work. Of a given morning, I'll hunker at the desk with a yellow legal pad, a sharp number-two pencil, and a stack of books. That is to say, even as I prepare to write, I am first prepared to read. The yellow pad is ready and available, but the conversation begins with my poring over the mentor's book, attending—word by word, line by line, sentence by sentence—to what has been offered to me on a prior page.

Here too, you might squander an opportunity if you are overly concerned with observing only what has been—as the Philistines like to say—*intended*. If you don't read strenuously enough, you may not be reading at all—that is, you may not be reading the way a poet reads. You needn't take my word for it; in his famous essay

"Tradition and the Individual Talent," T.S. Eliot makes a good point about the potential of this relationship we hope to establish with those who have preceded us: "No poet, no artist of any art, has his complete meaning alone. His significance, his appreciation is the appreciation of his relation to the dead poets and artists."

Mr. Eliot asserts that, just as the great poets (your mentors) received and modified the writings that fed them, so too—if you are to succeed—you must receive and modify these great teachers, even as you read them, even as you respond to them. He suggests that your conforming to this their model requires that you not conform *merely*—you don't just copy them—but that you bring the matter of your own imagination to your lively and enlivening meeting with their words. He continues: "The necessity that [the new poet] shall conform is not onesided; what happens when a new work of art is created is something that happens simultaneously to all the works of art which preceded it." In this way, he suggests, we come to see that "the past should be altered by the present as much as the present is directed by the past," and that "the poet who is aware of this will be aware of great difficulties and responsibilities."

Among the difficulties is his coming to own the tradition that fed him and will feed you; it is not a matter of passive familiarity, but a matter of strenuous engagement and participation. It is a matter of communion. Also among the responsibilities is his realizing that this activity isn't, finally, about him (or you) at all; it is about us.

FURTHER READING

My first inklings about how poems come to be poems probably began with my introduction (during my freshman year of college) to Samuel Taylor Coleridge's prose works, most specifically his *Biographia Literaria*. Something about the poet's premises regarding words themselves awakened in me a sense that words do more than refer to what is or to what was; they reminded me that words (as one witnesses in no less a text than Genesis) have the power to bring even a new world into being. Not long thereafter, I came across T.S. Eliot's *Selected Prose,* and in those essays and observations—in particular, his "Tradition and the Individual Talent"—I glimpsed something of the necessarily dialogic relationship that a young writer must work to develop between herself and those who precede her. About a decade later, these early hunches were further fed by Mikhail Bakhtin's *Dialogic Imagination,* Susan Handelman's *The Slayers of Moses,* and George Steiner's *Real Presences.* This power of words to provoke and to say (and to say and to say and to keep on saying) is not only discussed, but is beautifully performed in Heather McHugh's amazing essay collection, *Broken English.* Once one has acquired a taste for this sort of indeterminacy in his writing, and has thereafter acquired some measure of ability to perform that puzzling mystery himself, he can do a lot worse than visit Alfred Corn's remarkable book on the music of language, *The Poem's Heartbeat.* Should the poet want to experiment with a variety of formal satisfactions, Lewis Turco's *The Book of Forms* would prove a very likely primer.

Quotes from T.S. Elliot taken from "Tradition and the Individual Talent," *Selected Prose of T.S. Eliot* (New York: Harvest Books, 1975).

14

The Literature of Fact
On the Writer as Journalist

—•—

Philip Yancey

I stumbled into my career in journalism quite by accident while looking for a way to pay graduate school tuition bills. My work as a stringer for *Campus Life*, a magazine for teenagers, led to a full-time position as an editor, and that platform launched further adventures in writing. Although for the past twenty years I have worked mainly on books of popular theology, I approach each topic from the stance of a journalist, a fellow-pilgrim inviting my readers to join me in exploring a new landscape.

For the most part, writers lead a boring existence in which we spend our days in utter isolation, shuffling electrons around a computer screen or sliding a pen across paper. (Annie Dillard once observed that writers keep revisiting childhood because that's the only time they have ever lived.) Yet we of the journalistic breed have a distinct advantage: we can leech life from others. We may not pilot jet planes or croon before thousands at a rock concert, but at least we can sit in the cockpit jump seat or on a chair backstage and take notes, basking in the glow of those who actually do lead exciting lives.

As a journalist, I became so fascinated with one of my subjects, Dr. Paul Brand, that I followed him to such far-flung places as England and India and ended up coauthoring three books with him. We rode the London tube together, toured the Royal College of Surgeons, dissected armadillos and rabbits, tinkered with computer programs at a leprosarium. He even let me assist alongside as he treated patients under a tamarind tree in India. Yet I did not have to spend the rest of my life wearing scrubs in the daytime and scouring medical journals at night. In my search for a vicarious identity, I could move on to someone else's life.

Writers in other fields often view journalism as a poor stepsister. Marcel Proust sniffed, "The fault I find with our journalism is that it forces us to take an interest in some fresh triviality or other every day, whereas only three or four books in a lifetime give us anything that is of real importance." James Joyce proposed this condescending formula, "Literature deals with the ordinary; the unusual and extraordinary belong to journalism."

In the decades since Proust and Joyce, the ground has shifted. Indeed, a reader who turns from *Vanity Fair* and *Esquire* to the novels of Thomas Pynchon, Gabriel García Márquez, and Salman Rushdie might almost reverse Joyce's formula. Increasingly, literature has moved away from realism toward the fanciful and magical, whereas journalism focuses on the ordinary, the quotidian. And though journalism has metastasized into newly disposable media—reality shows on television, websites and blogs, MP3 downloads—it has also given birth to the field of creative nonfiction.

I resist that word, *nonfiction,* on the grounds that a major endeavor should hardly be defined by what it is not; we do not, after all, call dogs "noncats" or men "nonwomen." In my more defensive moments, I would suggest a moniker like "the literature of fact." Some university Associated Writing Programs acknowledge a new species of "factual and literary writing that has the narrative, dramatic, meditative, and lyrical elements of novels, plays, poetry, and memoir." That describes journalism at its best, as practiced regularly, for example, in *The New Yorker.*

Newspaper journalists have the singular goal of communicating information efficiently, hence the inverted pyramid structure that begins with the most important facts and moves toward the more trivial. The kind of narrative journalism that appears in the better magazines and often expands into book length has a very different goal. We are more interested in telling a story than in communicating information. I would summarize my writing goal in this way: to cause the subject (which may in fact be a person) to stand out in relief, in a kind of silhouette, for the benefit of a particular audience, and to do so in an engaging way that holds the reader's interest.

I have written for magazines as diverse as *Reader's Digest* and *Books and Culture*, *National Wildlife* and *The Christian Century*. Each time, I enter into an implicit contract with the particular readership, acting as their advocate or representative to investigate what I project as their possible interest in the subject I have chosen. Serving as a kind of tour guide, I strive to delve into that subject in a way that both engages and educates my audience.

⌣

Even as I am writing, I hear an inner voice saying, "That's enough theory, Philip. You're a journalist. Get on with the story."

Though I fell into the field of journalism accidentally, I found that it fit my personality perfectly. I was shy and socially awkward, and I tended to react to people and events after the fact, following a period of internal pondering and sorting—exactly the process a writer goes through.

Since I was writing for teenagers, many of my first articles developed out of interviews with kids who, behold, were even more shy and socially awkward! Very quickly, I had to learn some interviewing skills.

Tell me what happened.
"Well, uh, I ran into this grizzly bear."
And then what . . .

"It—she, I guess—kind of attacked me."

How big was it, or she?

"Pretty big, I reckon."

In interviewing teenagers, I devised a fill-in-the-blank method. Was the sun shining? What was the temperature? Describe the bear. Where did she bite first? Tell me about the pain. What went through your mind? Did you fight back? Did you yell? Did your life flash in front of you? In essence, I had to imagine the story (good practice for a budding writer) and then backfill it with the corrected facts I managed to drag out of my interview subject.

After I left *Campus Life* and went freelance, my range expanded to include an entirely different category of interview subjects: people of some renown who had learned to respond with canned answers. Bono, Bill Clinton, Billy Graham, Jimmy Carter—any question I might think up, they had already been asked somewhere along the line. As experienced public figures, they knew exactly how to fend off a probing journalist who might threaten their carefully protected image.

Once, while interviewing Billy Graham, I felt a sudden wave of sympathy for him and others under constant public scrutiny. If I were to ask, "Mr. Graham, honestly, off the record, could you tell me what you really think about gay rights, or the tricky issues surrounding abortion?" I'm not sure he could truly answer. He had learned over the years what to say and what not to say, and in matters of controversy his public persona had swallowed up his private person. He *couldn't* think certain things, and if he did, he certainly wouldn't tell some nosy journalist.

Every journalist who deals with famous people faces this barrier. (The flea says to the elephant, "Shall we dance?") A few years ago I agreed to interview the novelist John Updike onstage at a writer's conference. I spent a week studying some two hundred interviews he had given, and carefully crafted my questions to pry into the cracks he had left unfilled. But as we sat before a crowd of several thousand of his fans, when the eloquent and erudite novelist responded to my questions, guess who controlled the content? No matter what I asked, he steered his answers toward more comfortable waters.

If I want something more than other journalists have pried from a public person, I must somehow establish a position of strength. A few journalists do so by direct confrontation. The famous Italian journalist Orianni Falacci made her reputation by badgering and sometimes insulting her subjects. As she once said, "I'm not an interviewer, I'm a playwright. I just get the person I'm interviewing to say the lines." That style worked for Falacci, but not for me (unless, of course, I was interviewing inarticulate teenagers who needed my prompting).

Instead, I developed a style I call the Columbo method. In the television show by that name, the winsome Peter Falk would soothingly win the trust of a murder suspect and then, just as he opened the door to leave, would turn, rub his tousled hair, and say, "You know, everything fits together except this one thing. Maybe I'm just dense but you said you were at the neighborhood bar that night, and, correct me if I'm wrong, isn't that bar closed on Sundays?"

Rather than direct confrontation, I often bring up criticism through the words of another person: "I see that the *Times* really roasted you for that speech you gave in San Francisco. They can be so unfair. I imagine you read that critique—how would you respond?" Like Columbo, I only expose my background knowledge when absolutely necessary.

Toward the end of theologian Francis Schaeffer's life, I accepted an assignment from *Christianity Today* to do a comprehensive profile of him. Schaeffer was living near the Mayo Clinic in Rochester, Minnesota, undergoing treatment for the cancer that would eventually take his life. Because of the fatigue factor, he asked if we could do the interview over three afternoons, rather than all at once. The first day, I felt completely stonewalled. His son Frank hovered over us, interrupting, answering questions for his dad, warding off anything that might seem controversial. The second afternoon went little better, and despite my best attempts I had gained nothing from my questions but prepackaged speeches. Desperate, I used a Columbo-like subterfuge. I left behind a published article containing scathing criticism of the elder Schaeffer, with many of my notes and questions penciled in the margin. I thought if he saw that marked-up piece and realized that, as a writer, I had the power to slant my profile any way I wanted, perhaps he would take my questions more seriously. It worked. The next afternoon, for the first time, Schaeffer seemed genuinely to listen to my questions and give thoughtful, authentic replies.

Janet Malcolm, a journalist for *The New Yorker,* has written about the sense of betrayal that may steal in between the journalist and his or her subject. "The subject becomes a kind of child of the writer, regarding him as a permissive, all-accepting, all-forgiving mother, and expecting that the book will be written by her. Of course, the book is written by the strict, all-noticing, unforgiving father." I experienced this tendency often enough that gradually I moved away from the kind of investigative journalism that leads to misunderstandings and betrayal. I decided instead to invest my time in people I wanted to learn from positively. The book *Soul Survivor* includes the resulting profiles of some of these people: Dr. Paul Brand, Dr. Robert Coles, Annie Dillard, Henri Nouwen, Dr. C. Everett Koop, Frederick Buechner.

Good journalism, whether thematic or based on interviews, tells a story. As novelist and essayist Reynolds Price says, "The need to tell and hear stories is the second most important need after food. People are going to tell stories." And participatory journalism affords me a chance to live a story before I tell it.

Early in my career with *Campus Life,* I met a young man named Peter Jenkins at a writers' conference as he was working on the book

A Walk Across America. As he recounted some of his adventures on
a long walk across the country, he said, "I get tired of these reporters
flying down from New York, renting a car, then driving out to meet
me. They hit the electric window button of their air-conditioned car,
lean out, and ask, 'So, Peter, what's it like to walk across America?'
I'd like a reporter to walk with me for a while!" Thoughtlessly, I
volunteered. Even more thoughtlessly, I agreed to join him in Texas
during what turned out to be the hottest summer on record.

For several days Peter and I hiked together, swatted fire ants,
bargained with farmers for watermelon, chased snakes (and were
chased by them), and endured the abuse of cruising Texas teenagers
who had nothing better to do than harass the outsiders setting up
tents in their town. I collected far more material in those days than I
could ever include in an article. To complicate matters, Peter gave me a
manuscript of more than two hundred single-spaced pages recounting
his experiences along the road before Texas.

Several weeks later, I flew to Washington, D.C., to sort through
several thousand photos that Peter had taken and was storing at the
offices of *National Geographic.* That magazine's two-part write-up on
Peter's walk had attracted a higher reader response than any article in
their history. "How in the world did you decide on what to use from
the mass of material Peter had written?" I asked the editor.

"It's like this," he replied. "I went home early, sat down with a
beer, and read all two hundred pages as fast as I could." Then I put
the manuscript down, drank another couple of beers, and fixed a
barbecue dinner for my family. I went to bed early that night, got up,
and made some coffee. Then as I sat at the breakfast table I made a
list of the scenes from the book that stood out in my memory. Those
are the very scenes that made it into the article."

Though I don't necessarily recommend the libations, I did learn an
important lesson that day. Often we journalists slip into the "strict,
all-noticing, unforgiving father" role and want to write about weighty

matters of significance. Most readers want stories. Several times in my young career, I sat with other editors and colleagues during coffee break and recounted entertaining incidents from my writing assignments. One droll editor would come to my office later and say, "Philip, that was a great story you told at coffee break. Why isn't it in your article?" I began to think of myself as carrying a tiny video camera on my shoulder as I gathered material for my articles. I learned to assume that what catches my eye, what interests me enough to recount the scene to my wife and friends, is a good clue into what might interest my readers.

Before I turned away from investigative journalism, I visited the PTL Club at the height of its prosperity in the late 1970s. Jim Bakker claimed that God had revealed to him the architectural plans for a television studio complex in the form of a miniature version of colonial Williamsburg, and he proceeded to build just that. As he and his wife, Tammy Faye, tearfully pled for funds to support their enterprise during their television program, donors (many of them elderly and needy themselves) would cash in their life savings or mail in their wedding rings. Meanwhile, the Bakkers lived lavishly. They once held a wedding ceremony for a poodle and a Yorkshire terrier, complete with bridal gown and tuxedo, and installed them in an air-conditioned doghouse. Because I represented *Christianity Today*, the PTL Club gave me the run of the place, letting me interview employees and even volunteer for the telephone lines to counsel call-in viewers. I faced ethical dilemmas in writing that article, but in the end decided that my primary responsibility was to inform my readers about what was going on behind the scenes. (Bakker was later imprisoned for defrauding contributors and, to his credit, wrote a book with a title that says it all: *I Was Wrong*.)

Some journalists specialize in participatory journalism. George Plimpton courageously donned a Detroit Lions uniform and got himself knocked silly as an NFL quarterback. John McPhee took a raft trip down the Colorado River with both the head of the Sierra Club and his arch-foe, a builder of gigantic dams. When I read their journalistic accounts, I see them as my representatives, my surrogates who go places I will never go and do things I will never do. Through them, I live vicariously.

In order to make the leap from participatory experience to the reader's interest, the journalist needs to find a narrative drive, a force somewhat like gravity that pulls the reader from the beginning to the end. Sometimes what takes place inside the writer supplies that narrative drive. The story unfolds internally: the feeling of guilt and helplessness as I stood in a refugee camp swarming with sixty thousand Somalis waiting for food while I strolled around snapping pictures; the sense of astonishment when I watched through a window on Red Square as the flag of the Soviet Union came down and the flag of Russia, banned for seven decades, rose to replace it; the prickly sensation of fear as I challenged the African-American leader John Perkins to prove to me that racism was still alive in Mississippi and we entered a never-before-integrated restaurant and every white patron fell silent and left their seats to avoid eating with us.

Recently, I read a striking article in *The Atlantic* by a mother who wondered about the vulnerability of children in the age of cyberspace. She went on the social networking Internet site MySpace and picked at random a girl named Jenna. Without much trouble, she tracked down Jenna's school, learned her interests and daily routine, and found herself stopping by Jenna's favorite hangouts, hoping to catch sight of her. A perfectly harmless and responsible mother found out how easily a predator could prey on her own daughter. In doing so, she evoked, even personified, the fears of readers concerned about their own children.

In another example of the writer supplying his own narrative drive, I read a powerful account by an Israeli journalist who visited Palestinian refugee camps. As their guest, he listened to stories of brutality from refugees who had no idea that he also served as a member of the Israeli army reserves and had himself participated in such raids. They told of beatings, of late-night searches by armored soldiers shining flashlights into their eyes, of Israeli bulldozers destroying their homes. These are the new Jews, he thought to himself—an uprooted and despised people yearning for their homeland—an astonishing admission for an Israeli soldier.

An inner tension lies at the heart of each of these pieces of journalism. In the act of reading, that tension gets transferred from the writer to the readers, who are moved to a place of discomfort and recognition. The struggle, the *irresolution* in the writer provides much of the narrative drive. And that may be one reason why propagandists, whether religious or political, produce so much feckless journalism: they perceive the dynamic as existing between the message, accepted in advance, and the unconverted reader. They forfeit the power of suspense and momentum that propels good journalism.

Narrative drive need not always come from the writer's inner dynamic. Think of the flood of articles that appeared after September 11, 2001. We the readers supplied the dynamic in our confusion and our thirst for any facts or insights related to that momentous event.

Sometimes an exterior setting provides the narrative drive. One of my most memorable journalistic adventures took place in a forest in northern Wisconsin. A prison ministry cooked up a scheme to send a dozen juvenile delinquents and a dozen federal prisoners on an Outward Bound–type week in the wilderness, and I went along to record the results. For the juveniles, the experiment proved spectacularly successful. Loud-mouthed bullies were exposed as whining crybabies as the leaders made them rappel off a hundred-foot cliff or run a marathon. For the prisoners, the experiment proved a spectacular failure. If a federal prisoner who is six-foot-eight and two-hundred and fifty pounds doesn't want to wind a rope around his waist and step off a cliff, there is nothing that the most highly skilled wilderness guides in the world can do to make him do it. In this case, natural surroundings were the focus of the article, providing the dynamic that at once melted the juveniles and hardened the adult prisoners.

On international trips I have often encountered situations in which *irony* provides the narrative drive for what I write. One memorable night in Chile, I ate dinner with representatives of Prison Fellowship International in one of Santiago's finest restaurants. The restaurant presented a floor show based on Easter Island themes, and soon the stage was alive with beautiful women dressed in brightly colored skirts and coconut-husk bikini tops. Shouting through translators over the din, we tried to discuss prison policy and human rights with government officials in bedecked uniforms responsible for the torture of prisoners under General Pinochet.

On the same trip, I had a gourmet dinner in a restaurant in Lima, Peru. I have rarely eaten such delicious food and in such a splendid setting, a former colonial palace. Unexpectedly, the inside cover of the menu began with the words, "Jesus lives! For this we are happy." And as we ate, the waitresses appeared together to sing a vespers hymn for their patrons. The restaurant, it turned out, was run by an order of nuns who cooked, waited on tables, scrubbed floors, and worshiped, and did all these things to the glory of God. But these nuns introduced a modern twist to the Brother Lawrence style: they proffered gourmet meals in order to serve the poor of Lima. All proceeds from the restaurant went to fund their social programs among the poor of Lima.

When I returned to the United States, I badly wanted to write an article in which I brought together four men who were having a profound impact on world hunger and poverty. These four headed Christian relief and development agencies, and all four would qualify as obese by any standard. I wanted to invite them to a gourmet meal at a restaurant nearby and describe course by course the delicacies served us, even as I had them describe the scenes of starvation they had seen around the world. I never wrote that article, perhaps wisely, but the scenes in Chile and Peru and the imagined dinner in the United States all point to harsh ironies from which we cannot escape. In our upside-down world, that which most helps the oppressed and suffering often begins with a stab of conscience in those who know little of either. In some articles, the underlying context itself makes the point.

⟜

Meanwhile, the deepest irony traces back to the very heart of journalism. It is, after all, an act of vicariousness that leeches life from others and inevitably distorts it in the process. I don't lead prisoners and juvenile delinquents through the wilderness, or minister to prisoners in Chile or squatters in Peru. When it comes to issues like world poverty and justice, I contribute vicariously, by shining a spotlight on those who serve on the front lines. I rage against injustice by sitting in my Colorado office moving electrons around on a screen and arranging words and phrases.

Moreover, I never get it right; none of us journalists do. The act of writing involves selection, editing, point of view. When I report on a trip, I cannot include every detail of every person I meet, every conversation, every complexity. I choose, and as I do so I reduce my experience to what fits within the page requirements I've been given, as seen through my filter.

I love my work and cannot imagine doing anything else. I begin, however, with a deep sense of humility, an awareness that we writers are little more than Peeping Toms at the keyhole of reality. James Agee, in *Let Us Now Praise Famous Men,* wrote openly of the humility he felt attempting to do justice to the lives of the rural poor:

In a novel, a house or person has his meaning, his existence, entirely through the writer. Here, a house or a person has only the most limited of his meaning through me: his true meaning is much huger. It is that he *exists,* in actual being, as you do and as I do, and as no character of the imagination can possibly exist. His great weight, mystery, and dignity are in this fact. As for me, I can tell you of him only what I saw, only so accurately as in my terms I know how: and this in turn has its chief stature not in any ability of mine but in the fact that I too exist, not as a work of fiction, but as a human being.

Agee has pinpointed the essential difference between fiction and journalism. Fiction creates a universe and characters that exist only on the page and in the author's mind. Journalism has the audacity to record on the page what purports to be real, but is actually a reduction of the real as told through one person's limited point of view.

This truth struck me with great force when I wrote about a friend of mine named Larry, one of the most fascinating people I've ever known. A bisexual, he has a history of liaisons with individuals of both genders. A recovering alcoholic, he attends AA sessions almost daily, has twenty years of sobriety behind him, and has gone on to become a substance abuse counselor for others. Raised Mennonite, he rebelled by serving in Vietnam, but has since become a doctrinaire pacifist. Along the way, Larry became a Christian. He says he was converted by two hymns, "Just As I Am," and "Amazing Grace." As he heard the words of those hymns, it sunk in for the first time that God really did want him just as he was; God's grace was that amazing. In his own way, Larry has been following God ever since. Larry states his dilemma this way, "I guess I'm caught somewhere between 'Just as I am' and 'Just as God wants me to be.'"

I wrote about Larry briefly in the introduction to an article for *Christianity Today.* I changed a few details, including his name and location, hoping he would not come across the article and recognize my caricature of him. A few weeks later I got a phone call from my friend. "I saw the article," he said. I waited. And then came these devastating words: "Philip, I've lived all my life trying to be a real person, a three-dimensional person. You've reduced me to a two-paragraph illustration."

Larry was right, of course. At that moment I realized he had identified what we writers do, especially those of us who dabble in "the literature of fact": we reduce. We reduce the magnificence of human beings to statistics, and illustrations, and article leads. Journalism—and indeed all art—is not reality but a mere portrayal or depiction that will never do it justice. I try to remind myself of that every time I turn to the keyboard. I will do my best to render truth, but I will fail. I will never get it right. That, too, is part of the pilgrim journey of this calling.

FURTHER READING

There are many books that describe the interviewing process, by such professionals as Larry King, Barbara Walters, and Oprah Winfrey. As a kind of case study I recommend *Bono: In Conversation with Michka Assayas,* a fascinating, book-length encounter between an agnostic French journalist and the rock star from the band U2, an activist Christian who talks openly about his faith.

John McPhee, Malcolm Gladwell, and James Fallows are superb journalists who raise the craft to an art form. McPhee's *Encounters with the Archdruid* captures his participatory style of journalism at its best.

In terms of making the ordinary sound extraordinary, I know no better example than a slim, little-known book by Annie Dillard, *Encounters with Chinese Writers.* Though her descriptions of 1980s China are badly dated, she shows the novelist's ability to turn a boring meeting into a suspense-filled narrative.

Quote from James Agee, *Let Us Now Praise Famous Men* (New York: Houghton Mifflin, 1980), p.12.

15

Made Visible and Plain
On Spiritual Writing

—•—

Richard J. Foster

Heather Shamaine was nothing if not ambitious. Entrepreneurial to the nth degree. So it was no surprise when she decided to learn the jade business. Determined to learn how to distinguish superior jade from its many inferior counterparts, she went to a recognized master in jade. She asked to be taught by him and was thrilled to receive a positive response. "It will, however, be expensive. Twenty lessons, two hours each, two thousand dollars per session." Yes, the price was steep, but Heather, wanting to learn from the best, agreed.

She was expecting detailed lectures on the mineral makeup of nephrite and jadeite and more. What she got was vastly different. At the first session, the master teacher walked in to the room with two substantial pieces of jade. Lifting his left hand slightly he said softly, "This is inferior jade." "This," he signaled with his right, "is superior jade." Placing both pieces into her hands he turned and left the room, leaving Heather to stare at the jade. For two hours.

The next session was exactly the same. And the next and the next . . . for nineteen sessions. Frustrated beyond all imagining, Heather brought her lawyer with her to the final session, determined to sue the jade master for breach of contract. This time the master walked in with a single piece of jade, and, without a word, placed it in Heather's hands, turned, and left the room.

Heather Shamaine simply exploded. "You see what he does?" she fumed to her lawyer. "Every session he walks in with some jade, tells me one is an inferior piece and one superior, and then leaves the room. That's it! And today he doesn't say anything. Not one word. And this time he brings in only one piece of jade and plops it in my lap and leaves . . . and anyone can tell that it's an inferior piece!" Taking a long breath and looking directly at Heather, the lawyer replied, "Don't sue."

Now, this little parable offers us a path to understanding spiritual writing—the jade, as it were. Extended exposure to it enables us to recognize instinctively the genuine from the shoddy and the slipshod. Bona fide life in the kingdom of God shines forth in all its unvarnished goodness and stands in vivid contrast to all things cheap and paltry. This is what spiritual writing does.

Spiritual writing is among the most expansive of genres. It covers the breadth and length and height and depth of human experience. Its subject matter is almost endless, for as it says in Psalm 24, "The earth is the Lord's and the fullness thereof." We might be discussing the varieties of butterflies or life in the Ozarks or any number of other topics, and it can all be spiritual writing if somewhere, somehow we drill down into the subterranean chambers of the human soul. *Spiritual* is an adjective that describes a kind of writing that seeks to get at the core of the person, the center, the heart.

Spiritual Writing Is Heart Writing

And, so, the first and foremost thing to say about spiritual writing is that it is heart writing. It aims at the interiority of the reader: the heart, the spirit, the will. Spiritual writing is highly relational. It is personal. It is in close. It is intimate. It is never at arm's length. Never. As readers of spiritual writing, people need to sense that they are being addressed as persons who possess dignity and purpose and freedom, persons capable of believing and loving and obeying.

With spiritual writing, we slide in close and draw people into the journey with us. Spiritual writing is participatory in the extreme. We write in such as way as to look the reader right in the eye and say, "Join me in this living, in this obeying, in this following of the One, as the book of Colossians words it, in whom are 'hidden all the treasures of wisdom and knowledge.'" With spiritual writing we hope to make it untenable for our readers to remain bystanders. Instead, we want them to feel drawn into the action.

Right here, however, we face a genuine danger. We never want to override or impose. The intrusive writer does not respect personal boundaries. To fail to honor individual identity and individual choice is to forsake spiritual writing. There is such a thing as the authorial spirit of hospitality, and in spiritual writing we offer it in abundance. We leave room for our readers to go their own way. We refuse to presume on a captive audience.

I am dealing here with the "spirit" in which we write. Gentleness, grace, charm—these are hallmarks of spiritual writing. Even when we say things forcefully we continue to give our readers space and freedom to take issue with us. Who knows, they may well be right.

Spiritual writing is formational. Always. It is meant to get inside us, to deal with the whole person—body and mind and will and spirit and heart and soul. It is good if our readers come away knowing more; it is imperative that they come away *being* more. Knowing truth is good; becoming truth is better.

There is a depth of encounter in spiritual writing. We sink down below the superficialities of modern culture, and there we pause and wait until a deep interior conversation opens between reader and writer. Our writing comes from the depths and it calls out the depths in our readers. "Deep calls to deep," declares the psalmist. And so it does.

This calling out places a high demand upon the reader. Spiritual writing requires spiritual reading. Eugene Peterson speaks of this in *Eat This Book: A Conversation in the Art of Spiritual Reading* as "a reading that honors words as holy, words as a basic means of forming an intricate web of relationships between God and the human, between all things visible and invisible. . . . Christian reading is participatory reading, receiving the words in such a way that they become interior to our lives, the rhythms and images becoming practices of prayer, acts of obedience, ways of love."

Now, some readers are not prepared for this openness into spiritual participation. Not just yet. I remember well my first encounter with theologian François Fénelon's *Christian Perfection*. A good friend, Gunner Payne, had urged this book upon me. Highly valuing his discernment, I tried reading this book, but after eight or nine brief chapters I gave up. I simply could get nothing from it. Some months later Gunner and I bumped into each other. And, once gain, he urged *Christian Perfection* on me, and so I tried to read it once again. And again. And again. And again.

This exchange went on four, maybe five times over the next few years. Finally, Gunner quizzed me about my method of reading. I had been trying to "speed read" this book under the modern assumption that the goal was to extract the essential information in the book so I could use it on appropriate occasions. Gunner helped me to understand that spiritual writing cannot be read in this way. He explained that speed reading is a recent invention that has arisen because many modern books are written to be read for skimming, for pace. But many of the old spiritual writers were densely packed and demanded slow, thoughtful, prayerful reading. And so Gunner instructed me in the ancient practice of *lectio divina* long before I had ever heard of the phrase. I learned from Gunner Payne to read with all my emotion, all my mind, all my heart, to read with every muscle, every nerve, every cell of my body.

As I said, spiritual writing is deep writing. But deep does not mean heavy. In our writing we learn to let go of the everlasting need to wax profound. Frankly, it is an occupational hazard of religious folk to be stuffy bores. No, spiritual writing contains a certain lightness, joy, gaiety even, at times.

The best spiritual writing comes out of the silence. As writers, we learn to be quiet and still; listening, always listening. We listen to God. We listen to people. We listen to the mood of our culture. We, in fact, do more listening than we do writing.

When I am engaged in a writing project, I allow space most days for a one- or two-hour hike in a canyon near our home. I am accompanied only by my carved redwood walking stick and a water bottle. In the springtime this canyon is filled with the sights and smells of columbine and larkspur, golden banner and Indian paintbrush. Now, however, it is winter, and in the winter earth tones dominate. Even the ponderosa pine is darker in winter, blending in with the browns of gamble oak and mountain mahogany.

The absence of leaf and flower makes the boulders of the canyon stand out in rugged relief. They are always here, of course, but in the winter they fill the landscape like giant sentinels. I like the rock—hard and durable. Often I will brush my hand over one or more of the conglomerate boulders, studded with stones, all cemented together by ancient pressures.

As I write today, a winter storm is howling outside, dropping (the meteorologist claims) some eight inches of snow before the day is over. Even at six in the morning it is well on its way toward that goal. So, tomorrow, when the storm has passed, I will hike down in the canyon. Likely I will not see another *Homo sapiens*. But I will hear the Cherry Creek gurgling beneath the ice. In a strange way, its perpetual babble both calms and energizes me. No doubt other sounds will abound: chipmunk and squirrel scratching for food in the underbrush, and in the trees high above I expect to hear hawk and jay, American goldfinch and dark-eyed junco. I'm sure to find a great variety of tracks in the snow; a reminder that I have many more neighbors than I ever see or hear. And I will listen—silent and still. The poet Gerard Manley

Hopkins tells it straight, "The world is charged with the grandeur of God." In the silence of the canyon I feel something of this "grandeur." And out of the silence I write.

Spiritual Writing Is Incarnational Writing

Spiritual writing makes visible and plain the invisible world of the spirit. It is firmly rooted in the earth itself. Even more; it takes root in the love and terror and pity and pain and wonder and all the other glorious emotions that make our lives dangerous and great and bearable.

As writers, our first incarnational task is to be ourselves filled with this life we are talking about. We incarnate the life, if you will. By the virtue of who we are becoming we declare to all, "See, such a life really is possible." So, we learn to sink down into the light of Christ until we become comfortable in that posture. All these wonderful realities first work their way inside us before we ever write about them. Our lives are being formed and conformed and transformed into Christlikeness.

We are dealing here with the personable and the livable. We are constantly asking, "How does this life experience make me a better person? How is the interior of my character formed in new and fuller ways?" There is a lovely phrase that comes from my Quaker heritage to the effect that "our performance always needs to exceed our profession." And so it should.

We cannot, however, allow this important truth to paralyze us. We look for progress in the spiritual life, not perfection. This is as true for ourselves as it is for others. We do well to give ourselves a generous amount of grace and mercy. At some point we step out and write even though we are keenly aware of how much we lack in love and joy and peace and patience.

Then, too, spiritual writing is incarnational in the way we learn to stand *with* our readers in all their confusion and wonder and fear and joy and sorrow and hope and pain. In addition, we stand *with* them in their longing to pray. We, too, long for the ways of prayer. We, too, seek a deeper, richer, fuller communion with the divine center. So, with humility of heart, we become the interpreters of ancient practices for our readers. We stand between the sacred text and our readers saying, "Look, this is the way. Try it yourself." Spiritual writing is incarnational also in the way it cares for language itself. We handle words as treasure to be cherished rather than propaganda to be maneuvered. Words are the place where zeal and wisdom meet in friendship, in which truth and beauty kiss each other.

Unfortunately, today our experience of language is "after Babel." We know acutely the misuse and abuse of language. We look with sadness at today's steady stream of romance novels with their predictable plots and reality television shows with their bland diet of lust, greed, and power. In contrast, we dare to overcome the destructiveness of Babel by the sanctifying power of Pentecost. We use words to unite and heal rather than scatter and destroy. We use words redemptively. Gerald O'Collins, an Australian Jesuit, writes, "A theologian is someone who watches their language in the presence of God." So we take great care with our words, for they are meant to get into our bloodstream.

It pains me to say this, but most writing today—even if it is on spiritual themes—is not spiritual writing. It is not spiritual writing because it does not drill down deep into life. We see this thinness of writing even by society's very choice of words, where the cultural norm focuses on verbs with their quick action, skimming across the surface of life. In spiritual writing, by contrast, we focus on nouns that can anchor a sentence and help our readers slow down. This anchoring allows the adrenaline rush of modern culture to drain out of the reader's system. Now they can be still and listen, as we have learned to be still and listen.

Word choice is important. A deadened imagination lines the cultural landscape. We, however, strike out in a new direction. We dare to go against this tide of monosyllabic mediocrity. We seek to revive the imagination, to give the universal themes memorable expression. Our desire is to love words—to love their sound, to love their meaning, to love their history, to love their rhythm. We abhor the cheap sentence that prostitutes words for the purpose of propaganda. We are willing to hurt, to cry, to sweat in order to capture the great image. We are willing to take a phrase and rework it and rewrite it until just the right image comes forth, shining like true jade. This is the agony and the ecstasy of spiritual writing. There is nothing more demanding on a writer than the struggle for just the right image . . . and nothing more exhilarating.

I will always remember how as young children our boys were gripped by the succinct phrase encapsulating the problem of evil in C.S. Lewis's *The Lion, the Witch and the Wardrobe:* "Always winter but never Christmas." Instinctively, our boys knew that was bad, really bad.

Spiritual writing not only seeks the right image or the right word but also the right timing. We learn to wait, and wait, and wait. Then we speak the obvious just as it is building up in our reader's mind.

Not only in the content of what we write, but even in the writing task itself we seek to be incarnational. When I wrote *Money, Sex, & Power* I tried an experiment. Each day of the writing, I began with a time of meditation upon one of the Psalms, and in this way I read through the entire Psalter. My desire was to be baptized into the hopes and aspirations of the psalm writers, for the Psalter is the prayer book of the church. With the cadence of joy and beauty, worship and adoration that comes from the Psalms, I was able to look with new eyes at the issues of money, sex, and power. Each day of the writing, I also received Communion. His body broken. His blood poured out. For me. Thus, I was strengthened by a mystical life that was beyond myself.

From this worshiping center I began writing. My experiment was to see the writing itself as incarnational, sacramental even. I sought to picture God guiding my fingers as I put pen to paper (there were no computers in those days!). I tried to imagine God filling my mind with supernatural charisms of wisdom and discernment, as well as the gift of words. I envisioned God revealing exactly the right words to my conscious mind. In this way I was learning ever so slowly that spiritual writing is incarnational writing.

Spiritual Writing Is Risky Writing

One more thing. Spiritual writing is risky writing. This has various dimensions. First, without becoming self-indulgent, we dare to reveal ourselves. The personal nature of spiritual writing requires that we be self-revealing. Not totally so, however. God, in his mercy, gives us some experiences that are meant for us alone. When we share an experience or insight into ourselves, our readers need to sense that the well is deeper still. If everyone knows everything about us, we are shallow people indeed.

But, once we are clear to share about ourselves, we learn to share without being full of ourselves. In spiritual writing the left hand does not know what the right hand is doing. That is to say, we have moved beyond self-consciousness. This is no small feat, this sharing of ourselves selflessly. Indeed, I find that this only comes from the deep well of a heart that has been renovated by the greatness and goodness of God. We simply cannot program our own hearts. Only God can program (and reprogram as needed) the interior of the heart so that out of it flows "righteousness and peace and joy in the Holy Spirit," as the book of Romans words it. Only by God's deep, inward heart-work can we, as Philippians puts it, "in humility regard others as better than [ourselves]." This is the first risk in spiritual writing.

The second risk involves the courage to pioneer the way for others. Spiritual writing always has a prophetic edge to it. We begin by watching the culture carefully and discerning where that watching will lead us. Then we cast an alternative vision for life in the kingdom of God. For example, in a culture whose unquestioned values are excessive individualism and absolute freedom, we instead call for a rich community life together and mutual subordination out of reverence for Christ.

This is risky business, for it is quite possible to have the right vision but the wrong means to accomplish it. We can so easily run roughshod over people, treating them as objects to be controlled and manipulated rather than precious persons to be treasured. And more than treasured. But we take the risk in order to incarnate the gospel message into today's world.

The third risk we meet is rejection. We step out where others dare not go. In spiritual writing we inch out on a dangerous limb, giving voice to our own understanding of what the gospel means for the contemporary scene.

I remember years ago trying to wrap my mind around some of the writings of the philosopher-scientist Pierre Teilhard de Chardin. Three books in particular, *The Phenomenon of Man, The Divine Milieu,* and *The Future of Man.* His work in paleontology was certainly controversial, and I can tell you that his spiritual writings were just as edgy as his scientific thought. At the time of my reading, the criticism of Chardin was quite severe, even to the point of his religious superiors, the Jesuits, suppressing his writings. Yet, I prayerfully continued to read, and shared some things I learned from him with others—a risky move in an environment decided against him. Today, though, speaking to the prophetic role of a writer, he is considered an exceptional scientist and a great mystic.

Be prepared. Many today, like the scribes and Pharisees of old, are waiting to catch you and me in some defect or weakness, some controversy. Perhaps you remember the pain Jesus felt by the rejection he received in the towns of Chorazin and Bethsaida as the Gospels of Matthew and Luke relay. And if our Lord and Master was rejected, no doubt we will be too. That is the risk we take.

⌒

Spiritual writing has the capacity to transform the world. It alone speaks to the deepest yearnings of the human heart. When we do it, we invite our readers on a tour of life as it could be. We call out the deep-seeded, God-implanted needs of our readers.

We don't intrude upon our readers; rather we give hospitality to our readers. Using words that are vibrant and strong, with simplicity of speech, with our whole heart, we "rejoice with those who rejoice, weep with those who weep," as the book of Romans states.

As we rightly and fully engage in spiritual writing, we in some measure enter the sacramental mystery we see in John's Gospel of the Word that became flesh "and we beheld his glory, the glory as of the only begotten of the Father, full of grace and truth."

FURTHER READING

While there may be books on spiritual writing, I have not read them. To my mind, the best way to understand spiritual writing is to read the best of these writers throughout history, so I set forth a brief list for your reading pleasure.

I suggest you begin with Augustine's *Confessions*. It is the first of the journal/autobiography/memoir category and the gold standard. Watch for the stunning phrases he uses to describe the disordered love in which he was mired in his youthful days.

The Interior Castle by Teresa of Avila is simply the best piece of writing on prayer in the Christian tradition. This book positively dances with metaphor; it is really an extended metaphor, picturing the soul as a crystal or diamond castle. Nothing quite compares to its galvanizing, almost erotic, description of communion with God. If you like Teresa, you might want to go on to Julian of Norwich and her book *Showings*. Pay close attention to her image of the hazelnut.

The Journal of John Woolman stands in a class by itself. Watch how he agonizingly personalizes the issues of racism, sexism, and consumerism. Another Quaker piece, *A Testament of Devotion* by Thomas Kelly, is well worth your time. It is a book Kelly never knew he wrote, for it is composed of several of his essays that were compiled after his death.

Among more recent writers, I would commend to you *Letters to Malcolm* by C.S. Lewis, *The Return of the Prodigal Son* by Henri Nouwen, and *The Cloister Walk* by Kathleen Norris. There is a twentieth-century book that has just come back into print, and it is a treasure: *Letters by a Modern Mystic* by Frank Laubach. These letters, written to his father, describe how Laubach spoke with God night after night on Signal Hill, a convenient knoll just outside the town of Dansalan in the Philippines. All these books are fine examples of spiritual writing. I am quite sure that you will discover many other helpful examples of spiritual writing on your own.

16

Babylon, Babel, Babble
On Translation (Part I)

William Griffin

It's not global warming that's melting polar caps; it's global wording. Ever-increasing world population figures—from 6,676,937,292 in 2007 to 6,872,820,432 in 2009—can only mean more mouths talking, more languages invented, more hot air generated, which can't be good for polar caps or indeed for polar bears.

Babel

Of course, the population increase could also mean that we're living in a post-Babel society. According to Genesis 11:1–9, an uppity humankind was caught building a tower that would puncture the heavens. A venture full of pride of the worst sort, and deserving punishment of the worst sort! Hence, the pre-Abrahamic God decided to afflict humankind with a plague of tongues; everyone could still speak, but nobody could understand anybody else. Enter the first translator, smiling.

United Nations

In post-Abrahamic times we have our own Tower of Babel, a concrete and glass slab overlooking the East River in New York City. It houses the United Nations and, as of 2007, numbers 192 member states. Some 300 languages are spoken on the 16-acre plot. The official ones are Arabic, Chinese, English, French, Russian, and Spanish. There's a movement to add Hindi; another movement to subtract all but English. Unlike Babylon, translators lurk everywhere.

Suppose the Philippines wants to address the UN Assembly; the message will be in Tagalog; the words are spoken to an interpreter fluent in Tagalog and also in one of the six official languages; from there, the Tagalog message will be spread to the other five official languages; from there, it works its way to the rest of the member states in the chamber. Thus, through a daisy chain of simultaneous translators, with a time lag of only a few seconds, the diplomatic business of this world gets done.

Army Language School

Domestically, American foreign policy has always required a continuous flow of multilingual simultaneous translators. Trouble was, there were never enough of them at the beginning of each international crisis. In the 1950s Russian was needed; in the 1960s, Korean; in the 1970s, Vietnamese; in the 1980s, Chinese; in the 1990s, Urdu; in the 2000s, Arabic.

The Defense Language Institute Foreign Language Center, located at the Presidio, Monterey, California, is the Department of Defense's primary foreign language school. In 2006, DLIFLC offered crash courses in fourteen foreign, presumably strategic, languages, from Arabic and Chinese Mandarin to Urdu and Uzbeck. Alas, no Latin; apparently the Vatican is no longer considered an international threat.

Churches

As countries need translators, so do churches. The World Council of Churches, the Roman Catholic Church, even the Billy Graham Evangelistic Association need them.

When the Second Vatican Council began on October 11, 1962, bishops, archbishops, and cardinals assembled in the Sistine Chapel. The official language was Latin. Of course, all the prelates had personal translators who read Latin, but all the public addresses were in spoken Latin; alas, there was no simultaneous translation. In 1963 Graham's Los Angeles Crusade was simultaneously translated into five languages and broadcast on low radio frequencies.

Bible Societies

If Bible societies are any indication, the diplomatic business of the next world has just as amazing a story to tell. By 2010 the United Bible Societies hope to achieve an impossible dream. "An easily understood Bible should be available for every language with more than 500,000 speakers, a New Testament for every language with more than 250,000 speakers, and a Bible Portion for every language with more than 100,000 speakers."

As this chapter is being written (in 2006), there are "2,370 languages in which at least one book of the Bible has been published"; according to UBS that's "well over 90% of the world's population."

Wycliffe Bible Translators

Who does all the Bible translating? Wycliffe does most of it; it's an international organization of Bible translators "dedicated to seeing God's Word become accessible to all people in the language that speaks to their heart." The organization was named after John Wycliffe, an Oxford scholar, who supervised the first English translations of the Bible just before his death in 1384. In its seventy-year history, Wycliffe Bible Translators has been involved in more than six hundred translations representing seventy-seven countries. Today, Wycliffe's staff consists of six thousand personnel working in partnerships with expatriates and nationals worldwide.

Modes of Translation

Translation theory in the Western world had some noble beginnings. In a letter dated AD 395, Jerome, a monk, doctor of the church, and Bible translator, defended himself against the charge of mistranslating a papal letter. The specific charges were that he changed the salutation from "Honourable Sir" to "Dear Friend," that he hadn't translated the text word for word, and that he'd omitted some words from the original.

Jerome's first reaction was to find his accuser and have him brought up on charges of theft, fraud, and any other crimes and misdemeanors that came to mind. When he cooled off, he admitted he may have made some alterations and committed some errors, but they weren't willful ones. Such alterations didn't change the sense of the original, add anything to the original, or insert any doctrine between the lines. Further, in that letter he stated that literal translation didn't always make the original text readable in another language:

> Sometimes it's difficult to follow lines laid down by others; sometimes it's necessary to diverge from the originals; sometimes it's hard to preserve the charm of the original. Each word in the original conveys a meaning of its own; not every Greek word has an equivalent in Latin. To find the right Latin word, the right Latin expression, I may have to travel many miles to cover a short distance. . . .
>
> If I render word for word, the result will sound uncouth, and if compelled by necessity I alter anything in the order of wording, I shall seem to have departed from the function of the translator.

In his letter, Jerome quoted similar statements made by Marcus Tullius Cicero, the famous Roman orator, some four hundred years before, in the prologue to his translations of Æschines and Demosthenes from Greek into Latin.

> I've thought it right to embrace a labor that, though not necessary for myself, will prove useful to those who study. I've translated the noblest speeches of the two most eloquent of the Attic orators, the speeches

which Æschines and Demosthenes delivered against the other. But I've rendered them not as a translator but as an orator, keeping the sense but altering the forms by adapting both the metaphors and the words to suit our own idiom. I've not deemed it necessary to render word for word; rather I've reproduced the general style and emphasis. I didn't feel myself bound to pay the words out one by one to the reader, but I did feel bound to give him an equivalent in value. . . .

I'll be well satisfied if my rendering is found true to this standard. In making it I've utilized all the excellences of the originals; I mean, the sentiments, the forms of expression and the arrangement of the topics. As for the actual wording I've followed it only so far as I could do so without offending our notions of taste.

If all I've translated isn't found in the Greek, do know that I tried to make it correspond with the Greek. (Letter of Jerome to Pammachius, 57,5.)

From these two Latin stylists, Cicero and Jerome, have come the distinction between paraphrasal and literal translation.

Paraphrasal Translation

Ninety-nine percent of world translation, both spoken and printed, is paraphrasal. Simultaneous translation is paraphrasal by definition. Virtually all print translation—novels, biographies, poetry, plays—are paraphrasal.

"Anybody who has really tackled the business of translation . . ." wrote Bible translator Ronald Knox in *Trials of a Translator,* "will tell you that the bother is not finding the equivalent of this or that word, it is finding out how to turn the sentence." In another place he has said, "It is impossible to translate a sentence without paraphrasing."

C.S. Lewis was amazed at the New Testament paraphrase by Anglican vicar J.B. Phillips; "it was like seeing a familiar picture after it has been cleaned."

Literal Translation

One percent of world translation is literal. Most of that is devoted to Bible translation. The fingers of God seem to have played a part in the composition of the original texts and, hence, God's fingerprints should be found all over them.

Prime virtue of literal translation is fidelity to the words of the original work. In practice, this fidelity applies also to the wording. That's to say, the translator should choose the most obvious (literal) wording, high in denotation, low in connotation. This presupposes that the biblical languages are more or less like each other and also like ours, and that biblical dictionaries are more or less the same.

My initial attempts at translating were decidedly literal. I soon discovered that fidelity seemed to be literalism's only virtue. Felicity was nowhere to be seen. But fidelity without felicity in translation can be a very mean virtue indeed. Happily, the most literal English translations of the Bible—the Douay-Rheims Version (1610) and the King James Version (1611)—have much festoonery and perhaps too much mellifluity. The most recent translations, such as the New Revised Standard Version, follow this tradition.

Practitioners of paraphrasal biblical translation would claim equal fidelity, but fidelity of a different sort; fidelity to the meaning of the original. That's to say, a Hebrew idiom may be translated by an English or American or Slavic or Hindi idiom. The paraphrasal translator generally lacks the biblical education of the literal translator. The latter, on the other hand, has virtually no education or experience in writing his or her own language. That's not to say biblical experts don't write books of their own. It is to say, however, that they haven't read, let alone written, a thousand poems or a thousand romances or a thousand narratives or a thousand plays in their own language. Hence, they are severely handicapped when they come to translate the Bible.

If one wants to know what the Bible says, one should read a literal translation. But if one wants to know what the Bible means, then one should read a paraphrasal translation.

If one wants to do scholarly work on the Bible, one should read the Bible in its original languages. Failing that, literal translations will do.

Has the ultimate literal—or, indeed, paraphrasal—translation been written yet? Each and every translation ever done has an expiration date embedded in it, a date by which readership has dwindled so low that the publisher will no longer reprint. We have not here a lasting translation, if I may so eulogize.

Every now and then, the literalists and the paraphrasists, usually at the annual summer picnic, get into a slanging match. Truth to tell, there's much to argue about. But there's more than enough praise, and more than enough blame, to go around.

Destined to Fail

All translations are destined to fail, mine and Eugene Peterson's (who has written the next chapter) included. They appear bright for a time, but they're really dim reflections of the originals. It's the originals that are the treasures, not the translations. Fortunately, every language has its jewels.

A similar sentiment has been expressed by Spanish- and Portuguese-language translator Gregory Rabassa. In his memoir, *If This Be Treason: Translation and Its Dyscontents,* he savors his success with a veritable piñata of Latin American authors. Ultimately, he feels dissatisfaction with every translation he has done, "even the most praiseworthy."

Aspiring Writers

"*Traduttore? Traditore!*" That's an old Italian proverb meaning "Translator? Traitor!" Alas, too many people from too many countries think the same thing. But I would rephrase the proverb and turn it into an emblem for all translators. "*Tradutorre? Salvatore!*" Yes, translators, no matter how humble their work, will out-Babel Babel, ban the babble forever, and save the languages of the world.

But that was three thousand years ago, and this is now. Far from considering many languages an affliction, we now consider them a blessing. God is being praised in many voices, many languages. The result isn't cacophony—it's polyphony. Humankind has turned the biblical affliction into a secular benediction by the great commission, go forth and translate. This is not a Samsonian, not a Promethean task, challenging the divinity; it is merely a Herculean task to harness the words of humankind.

So You Want to Become a Translator

Master the English language, the dominant language of the world in the twenty-first century. Read broadly in the language, listen to the best voices of your generation, view television, watch movies. Remember, translating covers all of life.

Master a second language or cluster of languages, and do the same kind of reading, watching, listening in those languages. Travel to a country where your second language is spoken and live there for a time.

Consult the wealth of information on translating websites.

Seek out writing programs, collegiate and otherwise, that give courses on translation.

Join the American Literary Translators Association.

As for finding an entry point, if you're at all serious about translating, you'll find a thousand of them.

Last but not least, one can certainly earn a living, even have a career, as a translator.

FURTHER READING

The would-be translator would do well to read Biguenet and Schulte's *The Craft of Translation* (1989) and Schulte and Biguenet's *Theories of Translation: An Anthology of Essays from Dryden to Derrida* (1992).

17

Word and Spirit
On Translation (Part II)

Eugene H. Peterson

The crux at the heart of translation is that language is inherently ambiguous. Language is a living thing; the meanings of most words shift according to context and tone of voice. They are not dependably stable. The only language that stays fixed, regardless of context or circumstance, is the language of mathematics and the computer languages derived from mathematics.

Mathematics is the perfect language for getting a spacecraft to the moon, essential for engineering a bridge, mandatory for counting money and calculating interest rates. But going to the moon, building bridges, and counting money don't use up much of the available store of words spoken or written by the human race in any ordinary day. And you can't say "I love you" in algebra.

A very small percentage of language is used to convey information as such: facts, numbers, data. Mostly, we use language in personal relationships, making promises, wondering and admiring, asking and answering, praying and believing, affirming and negating. And, this is significant, telling lies. The same words that are used to speak "the truth, the whole truth, and nothing but the truth, so help me God" are easily and often used to mislead and deceive. Not infrequently we mislead unintentionally—we don't know how to say what we mean to say. Ambiguities abound. Language requires interpretive listening. Translation is interpretation.

George Steiner, one our best observers of how language works, in his book *After Babel: Aspects of Language and Translation,* insists that "the cardinal issue is this: the 'messiness' of language, its fundamental difference from the ordered, closed systematization of mathematics or formal logic, the polysemy of individual words are neither a defect nor a surface feature which can be cleared up by the analysis of deep structures. The fundamental 'looseness' of natural language is crucial to the creative functions of internalized and outward speech."

It doesn't take much imagination to realize the complexities involved in the use of language. The only place that a word stays the same at all times is in a lexicon. The moment that it enters a sentence, various possibilities come into play. When the sentence extends into a paragraph, resonances proliferate. In a story, words work together on a vast scale, modifying, bringing out nuances, hinting at mysteries, building tensions, revealing the unsuspected, suggesting but not resolving possibilities. Often the listener or reader acts as his or her own interpreter or translator. Sometimes we need help. A translator helps us to read or listen "between the lines."

These reflections are of particular interest to readers of the Bible, the most translated book ever. Since most Bible readers are dependent on a translator, it is useful to know what is going on behind the scenes and why.

I was a translator long before I knew I was a translator. I was a pastor responsible for getting the language of the Scriptures, the word of God, present and understood by my congregation. These Scriptures had been written between two and three thousand years ago in the ancient languages of Hebrew, Aramaic, and Greek. Yet, in my preaching and teaching and conversation with my parishioners I used a Bible that had been translated into English.

I was a new pastor. I had just completed several years of intense study in learning what was in the Bible and how important it was. I was prepared to tell my congregation what I had learned. They seemed willing enough to listen. They showed up on Sundays and were attentive. During the week I would be approached with questions about something they had read in the Bible or heard me say from it. But it didn't take me long to find out that most of the men and women I was serving as a pastor, all of whom owned Bibles and could read them, didn't read the Bible in the same way they read the daily newspaper. They read the Bible as a sacred text written a long time ago, learning that God saved the Hebrews from Egyptian slavery and that the Son of God, Jesus, died on Golgotha to save us from our sins.

They read the newspaper to find out what was on sale that day in the Safeway and Wal-Mart, and what political and military developments had taken place in Afghanistan the day before. The Bible was good for their eternal soul, whatever that was. But the newspaper kept them in touch with what was going on right around them that day. The Bible was remote from the world of children and playgrounds, taking a night school class in business administration, and arranging for a vacation in Hawaii. They liked listening to me tell them what it had been like in Bible times. Some of them even took notes, but they had things other than Bible study to do.

So I worked hard at building a bridge across this cultural, social, and geographical gap—ancient Israel on one side, modern America on the other—by doing a lot of defining and explaining. I wished to make them at home in the world of the Bible so they could understand it. I defined words that they were not accustomed to using around the kitchen table, words like *redemption* and *justification* and *covenant* and *expiation*. I explained the world of gods and goddesses, kings and emperors that made up the background world of the biblical people. I gave them inside knowledge on the *real* meaning of the original Hebrew and Greek verbs. I was quite sure that if I could make them at home with tenth-century BC Hebrews and first century AD Christians, they would understand the Scriptures.

It soon became obvious that my bridge-building work wasn't working. They were pretty good students, many of them. They were interested. But there was no bridge. When they left the church on Sunday, they left the Bible in the pews. I think I did a pretty good job of giving them a working knowledge of Bible places and Bible culture and Bible words. But when they got home and went to work or school the next day, they were immersed in a very different world. The River Jordan, the village of Bethsaida, and Jesus' words from the cross were one thing; commuter traffic, their several workplaces, and the words of television pundits were quite another thing. And there was a "great gulf fixed" between these worlds.

I was treating the men and women who gathered in the church to worship God and listen to God's word each Sunday like students in a classroom. I wanted them to get it right. This was *God's* word, after all. If I could have pulled it off, I would have gone back to square one and taught them Hebrew and Greek to make sure they got it right. Knowing the unlikelihood of that happening, I compromised by doing a lot of explaining and defining.

It took me a while, but I slowly realized that I knew a lot more about the biblical world than I did of the world in which my parishioners lived and loved and worked. And I was far more interested in making them knowledgeable in the language of the Bible world than I was interested in becoming fluent in the language of their world, the language in which they did their work, prayed, and raised their families. I deliberately set myself to listening to their stories, observing the ways they used language, paying attention to what went on between the lines in their conversations.

I didn't know it at the time, but I was learning to be a translator. Much later I learned that there is a word for what I was doing. Students of translation observe that there are two levels of translation, translation within a language (intralingual) and translation between languages (interlingual). Most translation is intralingual: parents translating the meaning of the prohibition "don't speak to strangers" to their children; spouses translating "what did you mean by that" to each other. Less often, translation is interlingual: French to German, Greek to English. I had spent arduous years of study learning to translate Hebrew and Greek to English (interlingual), and then several more years teaching my seminary students to do it. It never occurred to me that once that had been done, it would have to be retranslated again into the contemporary vernacular of Americans (intralingual).

But that's what I found myself doing as a pastor, preaching the text of the Bible from a pulpit on Sundays by interpreting—"translating"— the text into the world they were living in, pondering a passage of Scripture with a man in a hospital bed who was recovering from a heart attack, doing my best to, as the prophet Habakkuk writes, "make it [the gospel] plain" to harassed men and women, over-busy and on the run, so that they might get a glimpse of what it means to live by faith. I found myself in the company of Philip, in the book of Acts, chapter 8, who interpreted (translated) the passage of Isaiah that the Ethiopian eunuch was reading, not because the eunuch couldn't literally understand the Greek words that he was reading but because he didn't understand the *spirit,* the inner aliveness, of the words. I was pleased to recognize a precedent for what I was doing in the thirteen Levites who translated Ezra's reading of the Hebrew scriptures ("gave the sense" according to Nehemiah's words) to his postexilic congregation in Jerusalem. These people had once known the language well but had lost touch with the world in which the language was spoken.

Thirty-five years of such pastoral work turned out to be for me a thorough schooling in translation work. When I received the assignment to translate the Hebrew and Greek texts into American vernacular, I was ready.

As I prepared myself for this work I realized that all theories of translation, the understanding of what is involved in getting one language into another, turn on an understanding of the way language works, not just finding equivalent words in the dictionary. Ronald Knox, an English Roman Catholic priest, spent nine years during the middle of the twentieth century translating the Latin Bible into contemporary English. Reflecting on his work, he reduced the entire topic of translation theory to two questions. Which should come first, the literal version, as far as that is possible, or the literary re-creation of the text into the language of the reader? And is the translator free to express the sense of the original in any style and idiom he chooses? He found that he could not answer the questions with a definitive yes or no. But they turned out to be useful in mapping the terrain in which he daily worked.

The first question, literal versus literary, turns on the polarities of word and sense, letter and spirit. These are true polarities; neither has any meaning apart from the other. Word and spirit necessarily coinhere. A word is articulated spirit, literally—in the biblical languages, spirit is "breath" (in Hebrew, *ruach;* in Greek, *pneuma*). Breath given voice through the larynx becomes word. A word that is cut off from the breath (spirit) that made it is dead. The Apostle Paul goes a step further and says that it kills ("The letter kills, but the Spirit gives life"). A word ripped out of the originating context of the living voice is not only dead, it is deadly.

Translation always works between the polarities of word and spirit. Word is what is said. Spirit is what is meant. Adjudicating the relation between them is a complex art. The translator works in an area of radical tension between the language to be translated and the language into which it is translated. For two thousand years translators, Cicero prominent among the early ones, have discussed the nature and difficulties of the work. Commentary and scholarship on the theory and practice of translation has accelerated in the past century. Eugene Nida, a leading voice in clarifying translation theory and practice, has documented a slight but noticeable shift by translators. They now give more weight to the idiom and imagery of the readers than to the context of the author of the translation.

Knox's second question, regarding the freedom permitted a translator in terms of style and idiom, was clarified for me in the setting of being pastor to a congregation. Several excellent authorized versions of the Bible that maintained continuity with the broad tradition established by the magnificent 1611 King James Version were already in place. My editor and advisors encouraged me to continue the vernacular freedom that I had developed with my congregation, all the while keeping my ear close to the ground of the Hebrew and Greek originals. They promised to reign me in if I got too free. The result was *The Message*.

My favorite letter from readers of *The Message* was among the earliest. It may also be the most significant. The writer identified herself as an eighty-two-year-old widow living in upstate New York. She said that she had twenty-two nieces and nephews whom she had supplied with Bibles all their lives, none of which, to her deepening grief, they read. The translation was always the King James Version, the one she herself had always read, the Bible that had shaped her understanding and obedience in the Christian way. She had recently heard about *The Message* and bought a copy, wondering if it might be a Bible that her biblically indifferent nieces and nephews might read. She checked it out against the King James in all the key passages she could think of to make sure it was sound. She gave it a passing grade and bought twenty-two copies. It was too early yet to measure the results, but they were reading it and talking with one another about it. "But" she wrote, and this was her final sentence after expressing her appreciation, "I am still reading the King James. I will always read the King James."

And so she should. She had no need of a new translation. She had spent a lifetime assimilating the syntax and cadences of the King James Version and would squander a memorable heritage if she abandoned it. But, and this is what pleased me, she understood the appropriateness and need of a vernacular translation for her nieces and nephews and welcomed it. There need be no rivalry between translations or translators.

FURTHER READING

The book that affected me most was George Steiner's *After Babel: Aspects of Language and Translation* (1975), but I'm not sure it's a good entry point for others into the world of translation. When I started to translate the Bible, Ronald Knox's *Trials of a Translator* (1949) proved to be a wonderful entertainment. My friend and sometime colleague in translation William Griffin has written an essay, "In Praise of Paraphrase," that gives translation, especially biblical translation, the legitimacy and dignity it deserves; the essay appeared in *Books & Culture* (2002).

Part Three

ENDINGS

18

After the Fire of Writing
On Revision

Diane Glancy

I think in terms of revision because I have been revised. As a Christian, I feel that I have started over and over, continuing one development after another. After reading scripture, or hearing a sermon, I have made adjustments in my attitudes and behavior. I see new ways of doing things I had not thought of before, or new ways of thinking I had not realized. I desire to be rewritten, so to speak. *Don't leave me as I am* has been a way of opening prayer.

I am interested in revision because my writing also is in the revision. Revision is what must happen for me to write. Writing is in the rewriting. It is in the revised. It is the necessary re-envisioning of the piece. In fact, when I write there usually emerges both a death and a resurrection. I begin a piece. I find it dies on the page. It isn't what I had hoped. It falls short. It falls flat. It goes nowhere. Then I find a new beginning somewhere embedded in the piece and start writing into it again.

At a conference once, several writers were reading their works-in-progress. One of them, Mary Hood, opened her bound notebook and started reading the words of a story she had written all at once— beginning to end. I was amazed that anyone could write that way. Just follow it like one long trail. When it came my turn, I read at least the fifteenth draft of a piece with arrows and mark-outs and additions in the margins. I write in a mess. A sentence here. One there. Fragmented. Sometimes a sentence that belongs in another piece. I work on multiple projects at once. Somehow it all gets sorted out. Restructured. Revised. Devised.

Mary Hood starts at the beginning and goes right through. I would like to work that way, but my writing begins with rowdiness. With distress and discontent. Out of the snarl, I work my way toward clarity.

I can write if I can tolerate the snarl and gnarl of the writing process. It is never clean. It is never under control. I'm usually involved with several genres, working on several projects at once—novel, poem, short story, play, an essay that will become a collection of creative nonfiction—each piece broken down in various stages of development. Lack of control is essential in the beginning because that's when the writing takes over.

My work is a continuing process of development. This thought belongs here. This one there. I begin by recognizing the thoughts that belong in a book and which book they belong in until they get where they are going.

There are books that have come quickly with minimal revision. I wrote *Stone Heart,* the voice of Sacajawea who accompanied the 1804–1806 Lewis and Clark expedition, in two summers while following the Missouri and Columbia rivers, listening to the journals of Lewis and Clark on tape, taking notes. What could she have said as they camped here or camped there?

At one point, the expedition neared Beaverhead close to the Shoshoni camp, where Sacajawea had been kidnapped as a girl. She was returning home. What would Sacajawea have said had she been able to read the words Lewis wrote on July 28, 1805? "I cannot discover that she shews any immotion of sorrow in recollecting this event, or of joy in being again restored to her native country; if she has enough to eat and a few trinkets to wear I believe she would be perfectly content anywhere." *Now wait,* I thought as I read Lewis's entry. *History itself is in need of revision in this particular case. Sacajawea did feel emotion. She was overcome.* I began to write, "You see Beaverhead, the place you are from. There is a storm inside you. . . . Your people are near, though you don't see them yet. . . . You remember your tribe. . . . You cross a small stream . . . and there are some of the Shoshoni. . . . You hear your own language in your ears. You hear it in the air. . . . You have returned to the place you were from. The distance in you closes." It is Sacajawea's voice that revises that passage, adding the missing material in the journals of Lewis and Clark. Since the beginning of the book, I had been with her voice. I felt the momentum of the voice build, carrying with it interpretation of their visit to the Shoshoni camp.

The voice kept speaking on after the book. Later, that book broke apart from a novel into a play. In the magazine published by the Autry National Center, where the play ran in the winter of 2006, I wrote an essay on the many steps of the writing and revision process of *Stone Heart:* "[The invited playwrights] spend the week hearing actors read our work. The playwrights, directors, and dramaturges listen together. After each reading, there is a discussion of the play-in-progress. Critical comments are the most helpful. This is where it doesn't work. This is where it needs to be tightened. This is where clarification is needed. After rewrites, there are additional readings. Then more rewrites, and more readings of rewrites." We worked on the play for two years before it opened.

Some of my books have taken years. The longest, *Pushing the Bear,* the novel of the 1838–1839 Cherokee Trail of Tears, took fifteen years. It started with the premise of taking many voices to tell the story. The novel is a collection of the voices of those who walked the nine-hundred-mile removal trail from the southeast to Oklahoma. While writing that book, I learned about the importance of travel. I found I have to travel to the land where the events took place. Land carries memories. It revises the piece also.

I also remember the revision that the publisher asked for. It did not involve much rewriting, but there were long passages marked out with blue pencil. I had said these things before, or they didn't carry the story forward. It was something I had to decide to agree with or not, and I agreed. I hated to lose those passages, but I trusted the editor, and I wanted the book to be published.

The subconscious also works to revise, to edit, to change, to add. In a poem about my mother's death, "Exegesis," in *Asylum in the Grasslands,* I had intended to write, "All those mournings laid one upon the other like flowers on her grave." But I mistyped, "moorings" for "mournings," and it added a depth to the poem. She had been a mooring, and that was what had been cut loose from the ground as the flowers had been. *Designs of the Night Sky* and *Flutie* are two other novels shaped (and so revised) by land, the section lines of Oklahoma in both cases. The novels are broken into fragments for the purpose of approach. I revised them into brokenness (of heritage) instead of wholeness. *Flutie* is written in short, numbered sections. The narrative in *Designs of the Night Sky* is interrupted by brief sections of history, myth, and dialogue that read as if in a play, the way terrain changes as you pass over it.

For me, writing is a continual reworking of the different elements: characters, plot, setting, tone, pacing, theme. Writing is a refining fire until all the elements come together in a unit. At least once a semester, I take a short story to class. I set it beside all the drafts it took me to get to that story. I show the class my folder of rejection slips from magazines and publishers where I sent out my individual stories and manuscripts of collected stories. I tell the class, I revise and revise and send the story out again and again. Until it doesn't come back.

I also found that revision has to respect the way in which I work. Often I use sentence fragments. I remember an editor trying to edit a particular poem, "Small Horse," in *Asylum in the Grasslands* into complete sentences. "Then the gate is up / the truck is start / and he is at the rodeo / ridden . . ." The particular experience of getting a horse to the rodeo did not work in complete sentences, or even correct poetic sentences. Revision brings the work to reflect the thoughts or intent it came from, even when experimental. A piece seems finished when what was in my imagination is there on the page. I also emphasize workshopping to my students. Making constructive critical comments on the work of peers develops self-editing that is a necessary tool, a tool to be developed alongside the craft of writing. For me, it is the vital part of writing. Years ago, I was in a group of beginning writers. We critiqued each other's work. I learned the value of receiving critical comments. And providing critical comments for others helps me criticize my own work. The editorial faculty is required after the fire of writing.

To edit my own work, I have to stand outside my work and look at it as an outsider. I knew the play *Stone Heart* was nearing its destination in rehearsals when I could watch it and no longer feel attached. It was its own piece. Its own being. That position of detachment has become a necessary perspective for me.

Revision often comes through daily living. I see an image while driving. Or in reading, I find something necessary to revise or understand a story. For instance, I was working on a play about the Fort Marion casts, the busts made of Indians who were taken as prisoners from Oklahoma to St. Augustine, Florida, in 1875. One of the punishments during incarceration was to be locked in the ice house. Where did they get ice in Florida in the nineteenth century? I happened at the same time to be reading a story by Paul Theroux, *The Imperial Ice House,* and found that ice was packed in sawdust and shipped to far places. Sometimes revision comes through conversation. I will hear something I hadn't thought of. Or I will follow a connotation to further development.

When I am in the process of writing a book, which means rewriting, I also rewrite individual sentences until they connect with the developing style of other sentences, until they react with variety, yet stay within the framework of the overall style of the book. Revision is always the direction of my writing, and may be as simple as a minor change in the structure of a sentence. In "The Coat," a story based on the Old Testament account of Joseph's brothers selling him into slavery, I had written two sentences: "Joseph was lifted from the pit and sold to the Ishmaelites. None of the brothers looked at him." I rewrote the sentences: "The brothers lifted Joseph from the pit and sold him to the Ishmaelites. None of them looked at him." The first sentence became more direct. The second sentence changed because the previous sentence had changed. I didn't want to use "the brothers" twice. The rest of the paragraph seemed all right. Then I looked at the two sentences again. I liked the first sentence, but added "the brothers" back to the second sentence. Once again, it became, "None of the brothers looked at him." Maybe this kind of revision comes under the heading of tinkering.

I also tinker with the sound of a piece, reading it out loud for the rhythm, especially in books like *Stone Heart,* where the rhythm of rowing the canoes is in the background. During the retracing of the journey, following the trail with the yellow stripes down the center of the highway going by mile after mile, another rhythm forms and contributes to the writing. I looked for sentence structure for the purpose of movement or expediency. The journey of Lewis and Clark was slow, but it was rhythmical. In *Stone Heart,* the revision consisted mainly of taking out words here and there to tighten the momentum, until what I heard in the inner ear was there on the page when I read it. It's important to listen to a piece of writing. I often read my work out loud. When it seems complete, I read it at one of my readings. I say to the audience, I am speaking this into being. Into existence.

Spelling, grammar, and punctuation are important. I am not always precise in that area, but my word processor provides some spelling and grammar hints. And I can consult books to clarify my questions or confusion. Editors make further corrections. I also have the added issue of using language in alignment with the remembered language of my father's people. There are cross-cultural issues and a sometimes purposeful skewing of language to fit the fissures. Fragmentation is important to my writing style, even if the style disagrees with what the books or my word processor tell me is correct. In *Stone Heart,* I used parts of two voices juxtaposed side by side, which makes the book harder to read. That awkwardness is important in what I wanted to convey: the convergence of two cultures that were not going to mix. The grammar check was busy underlining much of what I wrote, but I did not revise.

As I mentioned earlier, I write in a slur of words. When I'm having trouble finding my way, I often record the piece, several pages of it at least, and listen to it later, after some time; when it is cold, in other words. I sometimes hear the beginning of the piece in the middle of what I read. The scaffolding has to be taken out. Or some of the paragraphs have to be rearranged. The first ones appear later in the piece. After that, I move toward meaning. What is this piece about? Revision develops perspective. Just what is it I want to say? Just how am I going to say what I say?

Revision develops layers and dimensions. It gives the necessary depth. It gets to the heart of the matter. In an early piece, "The Germany Trip," in my book *The West Pole,* I talked more about the pigeons in Nuremberg than the trials: "There are pigeons in the square in Nuremberg. They eat off the cobblestones. The one I see trying to hold up his foot, sometimes squatting on the cobblestones. For all I know, they are angels and mostly they are kicked or pushed out of the way." I continued for another paragraph. On the third draft, I addressed the trials: "I was a child in another country, but I was alive during these hearings in this large, hollow, wood-paneled courtroom where men tried to establish some kind of rules—some kind of rational standards by which we could determine boundaries of behavior. We had to define the violations. Say these war crimes are inhumane. We cannot ever go beyond these boundaries again. If we want to remain human beings." But the part about the Nuremberg trails is still not as long as the passage on pigeons in the square. I suppose I saw the pigeons as Jews. Maybe I wanted something indirect to happen. I would have more to say now. After Rwanda. After Darfur, Sudan. After all the atrocities of the earth. I'm not sure legislation helps human behavior, though that legislation is necessary. It takes a conversion of the heart. It takes revision.

When I taught Native American Literature, my writing was in that direction. Now I feel a revision in the subjects I choose. I feel a move toward Christian themes and issues. Christianity itself is under revision. I am interested in Christian writing. Writing with Christ-centered themes. Writing from the point of view of Christianity. This vast—what is it?—religion with multiple denominations and extravagances and fussings for place. Even denominations are broken into subdenominations, some in opposition to one another. It seems we're all wrangling over how to interpret and present, sum up, and say, this is the way so far. How can a religion have so many toppings? Revisions. Some even denying the very basis of Christianity itself—that Christ died for my sins so that I could be reconciled to God by faith in the shed blood of Christ. That, for me, is worth writing. How to put faith in words. The difficulty of writing about faith without being preachy, opinionated, or sentimental.

When writing, I believe in the unchanging certainty of change. Donald Justice, quoted in the article "Psalm and Lament" in the *Writer's Chronicle,* said:

I am one who likes poetry that is difficult, up to a point. It engages the whole man; I am bound to it by more ties of association. One is encouraged to go on trying to get beyond the difficulties by a kind of confidence the poem arouses, probably because it looks carefully put together; or it looks brilliant and flashy; or it reminds one of admired passages and thus through resemblance borrows some authority of previous work. I want to give the name benign obscurity to this kind of difficulty, for there are plenty of other kinds which do not work this way, but only leave one feeling rather lost and helpless. . . . Though sometimes mistaken for it, obscurity is not the path to the sublime, but then in fairness you must add that neither does it defeat the sublime.

I think a lot about my positioning. My agency. I think about what that means.

I am bound to faith. I was born early in 1941, the year America entered the war against Germany and Japan. I was in my crib while Jews went to the ovens. I was in my bed when bombs incinerated Nagasaki and Hiroshima. I was a girl in the fifties, when everyone had a washing machine and a car in the garage. The great awakening of materialism, of commercialism. I was a walking wounded, not a broken home, but a broken connective. There was a looking away from one another, more than toward one another. I felt the margin of a life. The connected family was where I wanted to be. But, for me, home ground was a dislocator. Faith would be the family I had: the biblical characters who were as isolated in themselves as Dorcas in the book of Acts, who had to wait as Joseph did in prison in Egypt, who was strong-headed as Miriam with leprosy because she spoke against Moses' wife, Zipporah. It was not a childhood. It was lessons in being unwanted. Of intrusion. My writing became the road, the vehicle to explore, to reshape the misshapen. To face. To deal with. To transform.

Writing and rewriting are about finding voice. That term, *voice,* takes revision to define. Voice is when the imaginative being from your head is on the page when you read what you have rewritten. Your style of writing, the way you write, is tempered or revised by the voice of the piece. When voices come together, they form a third voice, which is the voice of the work. Which is revision. The writer, the character, the piece itself. It forms a triad of relational positions. The author's style is transformed by the character's voice. The character is transformed by the shaping of the author. The two together form a third. A third comes from the two. The voice of the piece that invites the reader into the wholeness of the piece, with all the parts of working, steaming like a pot of gumbo on the stove. The cooking that is the rewriting of the cooking process.

Martin Buber writes about the I-it relationship and the I-Thou relationship to the Sacred Other. In a small way, on the temporal level, the act of revision moves a piece of writing from the I-it into the I-Thou. For the purposes of revision, the same thought can be found in the book of Ecclesiastes: "Two are better than one; because they have good reward for their labor. For it they fall, the one will lift up his fellow: but woe to him that is alone when he falls; for he has not another to help him up. Again, if two lie together, then they have heat: but how can one be warm alone? And if one prevail against him, two shall withstand him; and a three-fold cord in not quickly broken." Perhaps this passage is talking about marriage. I have heard it read at weddings. But where did three come from? We assume it is husband, wife, and the cohesive unit, which for the Christian is the Lord, or the empowerment of the Holy Spirit. But this passage works for revision also. The writer and the writing are the two. Rewriting or revision is the third.

Bringing the third back to Buber: the third is needed for the I-Thou relationship. That furtherment. That revision that pushes the two parts into a third. The completion of the book or piece of writing. I suppose, after that, the triad continues. The book, the reader, the interpretation, which is a revision of sorts.

Recently, I was reading the poet Jorie Graham's essay "Art of Revising" in *New Letters*. Here she looks at Mark Strand's twelve canvases of preliminary writing for his poems. "It [his process] both is, and tracks, in each canvas, an attempt to rework the language of an incipient poem until that poem is achieved."

It is in the vital act of rewriting that I find and hopefully achieve the voice of my work. Revision, for me, is the act of passage through the nascent stages of writing. I often am reminded of the woman in the Gospel of Matthew who said, even the dogs eat the crumbs that fall from the Master's table. In revision, I find the crumbs of creative energy that seem to fall from a larger table than mine.

FURTHER READING

Here are some books with helpful chapters on revision:

Off the Page, edited by Carole Burns, W.W. Norton, 2008.

Story in Literary Fiction, William Coles, Authorhouse, 2007.

Now Write, edited by Sherry Ellis, Jeremy P. Tarcher/Penguin, 2006.

19

Offstage
On the Writer and the Editor

John Wilson

"Everyone and everything needs editing." So said movie reviewer Joe Morgenstern in his *Wall Street Journal* column for November 3–4, 2007. "I edit compulsively in my head—movies I see, stories I read, reporters I hear on the radio," Morgenstern confessed. "I enjoy the editing process, which comes after the hard work of writing is done. Editing is when you get to play with someone in the sandbox of language."

Ah! You can tell that those last two sentences were not written by a man who makes his living as an editor. The editor's work—like the writer's—runs the gamut from sheer drudgery to inspired delight, most of the time falling somewhere in between. In fact, much of what we call "writing" is a form of editing, often called "revision." When a novelist decides that a subplot in her work-in-progress has grown unruly, demanding too much space, she is making the same sort of judgment an editor might make. So, too, when one of those fellows who turn up frequently on the op-ed pages deletes the word *rant* from the paragraph he's typing on his laptop and replaces it with *tirade*, feeling that he's found the mot juste. (His editor, of course, may have a different opinion.)

Novelists who employ cowriters—James Patterson, for instance, a dominant figure on the fiction bestseller list in recent years—typically give their apprentices an idea to flesh out, then apply the maestro's touch, "editing" the cowriter's draft. But for the most impressive evidence of the blurry line between writing and editing, we must look to the Bible, proof positive that editors as well as writers can be inspired.

Many outstanding writers have been editors as well, and vice versa. Charles Dickens and T.S. Eliot were as different from each other temperamentally as two writers could be, but both excelled as editors. When Nobel Prize–winner Toni Morrison began her career as a novelist, her day job was at Random House, where she had worked her way up to an editorial position. William Maxwell, who for decades served as an editor at the *New Yorker,* shepherding some of the best fiction of his time, was himself a first-rate writer.

Editing as a profession—an art, a craft, a trade—is a rather obscure business, and perhaps that's as it should be: offstage, in the background. As readers, we mostly don't know and don't care what part an editor played in the finished work before us. That contribution may have been negligible. Some years ago I spent a very happy week in the special collections room in the library of the University of California, Irvine, where the papers of Kenneth Millar reside. Millar is best known as Ross Macdonald, the pseudonym he used for most of his splendid novels. Macdonald—let's call him—was one of the finest writers in the tradition of Dashiell Hammett and Raymond Chandler (both of whom, I believe, he surpassed) and one of the finest novelists of his time, recognized as such by Eudora Welty, among others. Yet, since his death, while he still is mentioned with respect, he has receded from view. He needs to be rediscovered, beginning with a selection of his novels in the Library of America. He needs the right editor to take up his cause.

The collection at Irvine includes many of the spiral notebooks—the sort I took to class during high school—in which Macdonald, writing with a ballpoint pen, sketched ideas and composed his novels. You can see lists of character names—some he ended up keeping, others he discarded—and questions he posed to himself about the plot he was trying out in his mind. By the time he wrote the first sentence of the manuscript, he knew pretty well where he was going. Reading these notebooks, I was stunned to see how few changes he made as he wrote, and how closely the draft of each novel resembled the published book, more or less verbatim. No editor had much to do with it.

On the other hand, we have the facsimile edition of T.S. Eliot's *The Waste Land*, the most celebrated and execrated poem in the twentieth century. Here it became fully apparent how decisive Ezra Pound's editorial hand was in giving the poem its final shape—much for the better. More recently, there is the case of Raymond Carver, another superb writer and, for a time in the 1980s, one of the most influential models for younger writers of fiction, both in the United States and abroad. Carver was sustained early in his career by the support of the flamboyant Gordon Lish, who as fiction editor at *Esquire* magazine in the 1970s published Carver when no one had heard of him. Those early stories had been very heavily edited by Lish, to such a degree that some credit him for the creation of Carver's signature style: "minimalist," critics called it, though Carver disliked the label.

In 1980, by then having moved to Knopf, Lish edited Carver's second collection of stories, *What We Talk About When We Talk About Love*, which was to become Carver's breakthrough book. Seeing in proofs the radical cuts and changes Lish had made, Carver wrote to him, asking that production be halted. What happened next isn't entirely clear, but the book appeared on schedule as Lish had edited it. The case has received attention of late because the poet Tess Gallagher, Carver's second wife and literary executor, wants to republish the 1980 collection as Carver wrote it.

What Gordon Lish was doing at *Esquire* and at Knopf was promoting a certain set of aesthetic choices—not a rigid formula by any means but rather an attitude, a way of seeing, a sensibility enacted by the writers he championed. Critics love to talk about "movements"—the so-called Imagist movement, for example, given impetus by Ezra Pound in the early twentieth century, or the "Angry Young Men" in 1950s Britain. In both of these cases, and most of the time in literary history, the notion of a "movement" is misleading, insofar as it implies sustained collective activity. But the rise and fall of "styles" and the communities that cluster around them: this is the story of writing, from classical Greece to the Tang Dynasty in China to twenty-first-century America. And editors are recurring figures in that story.

New styles and sensibilities emerge to take account of new realities, and good editors sense something stirring in the air. They tune in to that signal, clarify it, amplify it. In the 1930s, a handful of bright young men (and a few bright young women) were dazzled by the vistas that beckoned in an unprecedented era of scientific and technological advances. Yes, they were living amid a global depression, and international politics gave good reason for despair. Yet all this seemed less real to them than the future. They gravitated to the cheap magazines that published stories set on Mars and Venus, most of them execrable in quality and woefully short on science.

Enter John W. Campbell Jr. Only twenty-seven years old when he took over at *Astounding* magazine in 1937, Campbell was an editor of genius, distinguished above all by an exceptionally clear sense of the kind of work he wanted to foster. As memoirs from the writers he mentored attest, Campbell did more than anyone else to give direction to science fiction. He not only published most of the writers who defined the genre but also, as Lish did in a very different way decades later, created a platform for a recognizable style. None of *Astounding*'s stars—Robert A. Heinlein, Isaac Asimov, A.E. Van Vogt, and others—could be mistaken for one another. Each was a distinctive voice. Yet they clearly shared a sensibility that was picked up and emulated by other writers in other publications, including the fanzines that sprouted up from coast to coast, anticipating today's blogosphere. And all this, in turn, gave the next generation of science fiction writers something to react against.

As an editor and as a man, Campbell had plenty of blind spots. Gifted editors with gigantic egos—Campbell and Lish qualify on both counts—are vulnerable to delusions of grandeur; they begin to suppose that they are the hidden kings of writing. Still, their example suggests the power of editorial vision. Similarly, though in a very different arena, Carl F.H. Henry—the journalist turned theologian who edited *Christianity Today* magazine from its start in 1956 to the late 1960s—helped to create a space for evangelical thought during a period in which evangelicalism was in the process of disentangling itself from fundamentalism. Were it not for Henry's single-minded editorial vision, the state of the evangelical mind, famously lamented by Mark Noll, would be even more scandalous.

A current instance of editorial vision would be Dave Eggers: writer, editor, activist, and literary entrepreneur extraordinaire. Founder of *McSweeney's Quarterly Concern* and the *Believer,* book publisher, the man behind the annual anthology of the *Best American Non-Required Reading,* Eggers too has sponsored a sensibility that speaks to the moment, with influence ranging far beyond the enterprises in which he is directly involved. No cultural moment is governed by a single style, a single sensibility, but if you want to taste something of the distinctive flavor of the early twenty-first century, for better and for worse, there's no better place to start than Eggers & Co.

⌒

Thomas Lynch, the funeral director, poet, and essayist, tells of the time when he completed his first book of poems and wasn't sure what to do next. Given a list of thirty publishers, he divided the list into three groups of ten, each to be taken up in a successive week. In this pre-laptop, pre-e-mail day, he made photocopies of a small selection of poems and added a cover letter. One of the publishers in the first batch of ten was Knopf, and somehow, in his ignorance, Lynch directed his submission to Gordon Lish, who was in fact a fiction editor, not a poetry editor. Three days later he got a response from Lish, who said he wanted to publish the book.

Many aspiring writers are convinced that the publishing business is mostly a cozy club, arranged to keep outsiders out. On the contrary: wherever editors happen to be situated, acquiring titles for a publisher, presiding over the review section of a magazine, or otherwise exercising judgment, nothing makes them happier than discovering new voices. Their door is open, as it was when Gordon Lish read a batch of unsolicited poems by an unknown from the Midwest.

Still, there's more than a grain of truth in the dark suspicions of disappointed writers. Of course there is an intricate network of connections in the publishing world—or rather, there are many overlapping networks, which make it easier for the insider to get ahead. And editors, yes, are quite fallible, their decisions often based on reputation rather than on independent judgment. In the early 1980s, Doris Lessing, who won the Nobel Prize in Literature in 2007, played a little trick. She submitted two novels under the pseudonym "Jane Somers." Her longtime U.K. publisher, not recognizing them as Lessing's work, turned them down, though another publisher accepted them. They received very little attention and sold negligibly. After the fact, Lessing revealed the stunt, and the books were republished— much more successfully—with her identity known. The words in those novels hadn't changed a bit. But now that they were by Doris Lessing, not "Jane Somers," they suddenly seemed much more interesting, more insightful, worthy of careful attention.

Ideology and prejudice haven't been banished from our enlightened twenty-first-century world. Editors, moreover, are constrained by the imperatives of the market and by the "culture" of their employer, by assumptions about what fits their list, their magazine, their paper, by the sales history of the author whose work they are considering. Not all good writing gets published. Lots of bad writing *does* get published. So why not start your own publishing enterprise? That is precisely what Dave Eggers did. And, in a different way, it's what countless writers are doing these days, self-publishing in blogs and similar ventures on the web.

Joe Morgenstern took note of this development in that same *Wall Street Journal* column, suggesting that it's part of a larger cultural trend: "We live in increasingly unedited times," he wrote. "Movies grow not only longer, but more misshapen. Bloggers aren't edited, for worse as well as better. Kids resent being edited by teachers; they think it cramps their creativity. Broadcast journalists are edited for time, but seldom for clarity of content. Anchors babble and bloviate; unable to edit themselves, they can't ask simple questions."

Well, maybe. For instance, a lot of movies *are* bloated and misshapen, but movie *trailers,* designed to lure you into the theater, are edited with exquisite care (whatever the quality of the films they serve)—and not a few movies are too. In other realms, Morgenstern's intuition rings truer. Editing is expensive. Morgenstern mentions a phone conversation with his editor (in New York, while Morgenstern himself works from Santa Monica) about a single word in one of his columns. He'd referred to the film *Evan Almighty* as "inexplicably awful," and his editor wondered if plain "awful" wouldn't suffice. Morgenstern made a good case for keeping the modifier, and his editor agreed.

Remember, this conversation dealt with a weekly column in which Morgenstern typically reviews several films. It appeared in a newspaper, to be tossed in the recycling bin the next day. And it's representative of the kind of work that goes into the production of high-quality newspapers (an endangered species) and magazines and books. We are far from living in an "unedited world," but financial pressures—the result, in part, of dizzyingly complex changes in the media landscape, very much still in progress—are eating away, here and there, at the commitments that sustain painstaking editing.

Editors work with words, but they also work with people. My oldest daughter, Anna, is an acquisitions editor for a publisher of local history. With a few exceptions, the authors she works with are not academics or professional writers. They are amateurs, passionately interested in a subject (the history of a town, perhaps, or a baseball team, or an ethnic community) and often giddy at the prospect of authorship. Anna operates within strict constraints (the books must follow a standard format, for example), but within those limits she gives her full imaginative sympathy to the writers. What she does—what many editors do—is as much about paying attention to people as it is about the nuts and bolts of writing.

When I am asked how I see my job as an editor, I turn to C.S. Lewis's little book *An Experiment in Criticism,* in which he considers various familiar answers to the question why we should value literature—and finds them wanting. His own answer is that "we seek an enlargement of being." We are limited by our makeup and our experience, each of us different from everyone else, but we yearn for a more expansive view: "We want to see with other eyes, to imagine with other imaginations, to feel with other hearts, as well as our own." And thanks to our common humanity, reading allows us to enjoy this extension of being—so much so, Lewis adds, that we "delight to enter into other men's beliefs (those, say, of Lucretius or Lawrence) even though we think them untrue. And into their passions, though we think them depraved, like those, sometimes, or Marlowe or Carlyle. And into their imaginations, though they lack all realism of content." In this act of imaginative sympathy, Lewis concludes, "I become a thousand men and yet remain myself."

Something like that lies at the heart of editing as I understand it. My job is to tune in to the distinctive signal of this or that writer, to see the world as she sees it, to delight in her particular way of expressing herself. Having done so, I can tweak a few details—sometimes more is required—or suggest a useful revision. An editor should be keenly attuned to what Gerard Manley Hopkins called the "inscape" of each writer he works with, even when the work in question is on the modest scale of a book review. And at the same time, the editor needs to put himself in the reader's place, extending imaginative sympathy in that direction. Does this entail a complete suppression of judgment, a fancy way of saying *OK, whatever turns you on*? Not at all. But it does mean that, as an editor, I publish many things I disagree with. And it means I publish writers who differ from one another not only in their opinions on many subjects but also in the flavor of their sentences.

Editing—in my little neck of the woods, anyway—opens windows not only via contact with the irreducible singularity of other minds but also through the heterogeneous subjects it thrusts before my eyes, higgledy-piggledy. Detective stories from Sweden and Norway, Victorian popularizers of science, the life of Tamerlane, the poems of John Ashbery, the art of Stuart Davis, a concise history of *The Shawnees and the War for America:* what they point to is the sheer excess of Creation, the largeness of things, always exceeding our grasp, always more, more. "My own eyes are not enough for me," Lewis writes. "Even the eyes of all humanity are not enough. I regret that the brutes cannot write books. Very gladly would I learn what face things present to a mouse or a bee; more gladly still would I perceive the olfactory world charged with all the information and emotion it carries for a dog." Yes! Why be an editor? Certainly not for fame or fortune. But if you share Lewis's appetite, a hunger that verges on obsession, faintly ridiculous yet quintessentially human, what better way to earn a living?

FURTHER READING

Two collections of letters illuminate different facets of the relationship between writer and editor. *The Only Thing That Counts: The Ernest Hemingway–Maxwell Perkins Correspondence,* edited by Matthew J. Bruccoli, documents the interplay between Hemingway and the legendary Scribners editor who also worked with F. Scott Fitzgerald. "Perkins' editorial technique," Bruccoli notes, "was advisory and supportive—not collaborative. He did not revise or rewrite. He did not function as a line editor." But what he did provide was indispensable. *The Happiness of Getting It Down Right: Letters of Frank O'Connor and William Maxwell,* edited by Michael Steinman, comes from the world of *The New Yorker,* where every word was subject to scrutiny, but it is also a correspondence between two writers, since Maxwell—like the Irish master O'Connor—was himself a very fine writer of fiction.

The longtime editor of *The New Yorker,* William Shawn, was among the greatest editors of the twentieth century, or any century, his genius matched only by his neurotic quirks. There are many books about the magazine and the Shawn era. An affectionate portrait that gives a sense of how Shawn worked with writers is *Remembering Mr. Shawn's* New Yorker: *The Invisible Art of Editing* by Ved Mehta.

For advice on working with editors, see *The New Writer's Handbook 2007,* edited by Philip Martin, which includes a couple of chapters on the subject. Also useful in this respect, especially for academics, is the chapter "What Editors Look For" in William Germano's *Getting It Published: A Guide for Scholars and Anyone Else Serious about Serious Books.*

Doris Betts is the author of nine novels and story collections. She is retired after thirty-three years of teaching writing and literature at the University of North Carolina–Chapel Hill.

Scott Cairns's sixth poetry collection, *Compass of Affection*, appeared in 2006. Recent works have appeared in *Paris Review, New Republic, The Atlantic Monthly, Tiferet, Spiritus, Poetry,* and *Image,* as well as *Best American Spiritual Writing*. His memoir, *Short Trip to the Edge,* and his translations, *Love's Immensity,* both appeared in 2007. He was a Guggenheim Fellow in 2006 and directs the creative writing program at the University of Missouri.

Harold Fickett is the author of many books, including an acclaimed novel about the evangelical experience, *The Holy Fool,* as well as a critical biography of Flannery O'Connor, *Images of Grace,* and the inspirational *The Living Christ.* He is a cofounder of the journal *Image: Art, Faith, Mystery* and associate editor of the online Catholic magazine and member network *GodSpy* (www.godspy. com). He also writes regularly for *Books & Culture.*

Richard J. Foster is the author of several bestselling books, including *Celebration of Discipline* and *Prayer,* which in 1993 was named *Christianity Today*'s Book of the Year and won the Gold Medallion Award from the Evangelical Christian Publishers' Association. More recent is his acclaimed book *Streams of Living Water,* which seeks a balanced path to the renewal of the church. He is one of the founders of the Chrysostom Society and the founder of Renovaré, an infrachurch movement committed to the renewal of the church in all her multifaceted expressions.

Diane Glancy is the author of *Rooms: New and Selected Poems, In-Between Places: Essays, The Dance Partner: Stories of the Ghost Dance,* and *Asylum in the Grasslands.* She was awarded a 2003 National Endowment for the Arts Fellowship and the 2003 Juniper Poetry Prize from the University of Massachusetts Press for *Primer of the Obsolete.* Glancy's novels include *Designs of the Night Sky, Stone Heart: A Story of Sacajawea,* and *Pushing the Bear: A Novel of the Trail of Tears.* Her new book, *The Reason for Crows,* a novel of Kateri Tekakwitha, is forthcoming from SUNY Press. Glancy is a professor at Macalester College in St. Paul, Minnesota, where she taught Native American literature and creative writing. Now on a four-year sabbatical/early retirement program, she is a visiting professor at Kenyon College.

Emilie Griffin is a writer, editor, and speaker. Her sixteen books on spiritual life include *Turning* (about conversion), *Clinging* (about prayer), and *Doors into Prayer.* She is married to Chrysostom Society member William Griffin; they live in Alexandria, Louisiana. With fellow Chrysostom Society member Richard Foster, she coedited the anthology *Spiritual Classics in the Light of Twelve Spiritual Disciplines.* Her latest book is *Small Surrenders: A Lenten Journey.*

William Griffin is a translator as well as an editor, biographer, journalist, and playwright. Among his translations of Latin spiritual classics are four Thomas à Kempis books (*Imitation, Soliloquy, Roses,* and *Lilies*) and Augustine's *Sermons to the People: Advent, Christmas, New Year's, Epiphany* as well as a biographical anthology with excerpts from his *Teacher, Confessions, Sermons, Letters,* and Possidius's biography. At present he's translating the Apocrypha in preparation for a Catholic edition of Eugene Peterson's *The Message: The Bible in Contemporary Language.*

John Leax moved across the ridge from the Allegheny River watershed and came to rest in the Genesee Valley forty years ago. He lives with his wife in a hundred-year-old house and gardens at the edge of town. Poet-in-residence at Houghton College, he has written ten books, including *Standing Ground, Out Walking, Grace Is Where I Live,* and *Tabloid News.*

Erin McGraw is the author of five books of fiction, most recently *The Seamstress of Hollywood Boulevard*. Her short fiction has appeared in *The Atlantic Monthly, STORY, Good Housekeeping, The Southern Review,* and many other magazines. She teaches writing at the Ohio State University.

Keith Miller has a degree in business finance from Oklahoma University. He studied theology at Yale Divinity School and completed a theological degree at Earlham School of Religion. He also holds a degree in psychological counseling from the University of Texas. He has worked as a businessman, professor, writer, founding director of Laity Lodge, and as a speaker. He has written or coauthored more than twenty-four books. Among his best-known titles are *The Taste of New Wine, A Hunger for Healing, Compelled to Control,* and *The Edge of Adventure* (with Bruce Larson).

Rudy Nelson was chair of the Barrington College English department (1957–1967) and associate professor of English and religious studies, University at Albany, from which he retired in 1994. He is the author of *The Making and Unmaking of an Evangelical Mind: The Case of Edward Carnell* (Cambridge University Press, 1987) and coproducer of the documentary film *Precarious Peace: God and Guatemala.* He and his wife, Shirley, live in Amherst, Massachusetts.

Virginia Stem Owens has written more than seventeen books, including four novels and nonfiction works on a wide range of topics from media to metaphysics. She has been on the editorial board of *Books & Culture* since its inception. She also served for seven years as director of the Milton Center, an institute dedicated to fostering excellence in writing by Christians. Virginia lives in Huntsville, Texas, with her husband, David, a dog, two cats, and a varying number of chickens.

Eugene H. Peterson is professor emeritus of spiritual theology at Regent College, Vancouver, British Columbia. He is the author of over thirty books, including his popular contemporary translation of the Bible, *The Message.* He is currently writing a series of books on spiritual theology.

James Calvin Schaap is the author of several novels (*In the Silence There Are Ghosts, Romey's Place, Touches the Sky,* and others) and collections of short stories (*Paternity, The Privacy of Storm, Startling Joy: Stories for the Christmas Season*). In addition, he has written a number of collections of creative nonfiction, including *Crossing Over: The Stories of Refugee Asian Christians.* He teaches writing and literature at Dordt College, in Sioux Center, Iowa.

Luci Shaw is a poet, essayist, teacher, and retreat leader. Author of a number of prose books and nine volumes of poetry, she is writer-in-residence at Regent College, Vancouver, British Columbia, and travels internationally to speak and teach on topics such as poetry, journal writing, and the Christian imagination. Widely anthologized, her poetry has appeared in *Image, Weavings, Books & Culture, The Christian Century, Rock & Sling, Ruminate, Radix, Crux, The Southern Review, Stonework, Nimble Spirit,* and others. She lives in Bellingham, Washington, with her husband, John Hoyte. For further information, visit www.lucishaw.com.

Robert Siegel is the author of nine books of poetry and fiction. His poetry includes *A Pentecost of Finches: New and Selected Poems* and *The Waters Under the Earth* and has received awards from *Poetry,* the Ingram Merrill Foundation, and the National Endowment for the Arts. He formerly directed the graduate creative writing program at the University of Wisconsin–Milwaukee.

Dain Trafton was for many years a professor of literature and creative writing. He has published scholarly and critical works (on English, American, French, Italian, and neo-Latin literatures), translations (from Italian into English), stories (mostly set in the past), and one poem. Now happily unemployed, he lives in the western mountains of Maine, where he works on his fiction and poetry.

Jeanne Murray Walker has published six collections of poetry, including *Coming Into History* and *A Deed to the Light* (University of Illinois Press, 2004). Her work appears in anthologies and journals, including *Poetry, Image, American Poetry Review, The Gettysburg Review, The Southern Review,* and *The Nation.* Among her awards are the Prairie Schooner-Strousse Prize, an NEA Fellowship, *The Atlantic Monthly* Fellowship, and a Pew Fellowship in the Arts. Her plays have been produced across the United States and in London.

John Wilson is the editor of *Books & Culture,* a bimonthly review. He edited the *Best Christian Writing* series, the last volume of which was *Best Christian Writing 2006* (Jossey-Bass).

Philip Yancey joined the staff of *Campus Life* magazine in 1971 and worked there as editor for eight years before affiliating with its sister publication *Christianity Today.* His articles have appeared in eighty different publications, and his twenty books include *Where Is God When It Hurts?, The Jesus I Never Knew, What's So Amazing About Grace?* and *Prayer: Does It Make Any Difference?*

The Chrysostom Society

In 1986 Richard Foster had a bright idea. He wanted to gather together some writers to find out if they could accomplish more together than as individuals. His intention, announced in his letter of invitation to new members, was "to consider the feasibility of establishing a National Guild of Professional Writers" whose literary efforts flowed out of the Christian worldview.

Soon twelve writers met at Christ Haven, a retreat center in Colorado Springs.

From that time forward, the group has met annually. Members have come and gone, but numbers have stayed between twenty to twenty-five.

The group has included Baptists, Christian Reformed, Church of God, Anglicans, Episcopalians, Lutherans, Presbyterians, Quakers, Eastern Orthodox, and Roman Catholics.

The authors who make up the group include poets, playwrights, novelists, critics, biographers, and spiritual writers. In its early days, the group took the name "Chrysostom Society," recalling John Chrysostom, whose name means "golden-mouthed," who is among the greatest of the Greek fathers of the Church. Born in about AD 347, he died in 407 and in 451, at the Council of Chalcedon, he was declared a Doctor of the Universal Church.

ABOUT PARACLETE PRESS

Who We Are

Paraclete Press is an ecumenical publisher of books and recordings on Christian spirituality. Our publishing represents a full expression of Christian belief and practice—from Catholic to Evangelical, from Protestant to Orthodox.

Paraclete Press is the publishing arm of the Community of Jesus, an ecumenical monastic community in the Benedictine tradition. As such, we are uniquely positioned in the marketplace without connection to a large corporation and with informal relationships to many branches and denominations of faith.

We like it best when people buy our books from booksellers, our partners in successfully reaching as wide an audience as possible.

What We Are Doing

Books—Paraclete Press publishes books that show the richness and depth of what it means to be Christian. Although Benedictine spirituality is at the heart of all that we do, we publish books that reflect the Christian experience across many cultures, time periods, and houses of worship.

We publish books that nourish the vibrant life of the church and its people—books about spiritual practice, formation, history, ideas, and customs.

We have several different series of books within Paraclete Press, including the best-selling Living Library series of modernized classic texts; A Voice from the Monastery—giving voice to men and women monastics about what it means to live a spiritual life today; award-winning literary faith fiction; and books that explore Judaism and Islam and discover how these faiths inform Christian thought and practice.

Recordings—From Gregorian chant to contemporary American choral works, our music recordings celebrate the richness of sacred choral music through the centuries. Paraclete is proud to distribute the recordings of the internationally acclaimed choir Gloriæ Dei Cantores, who have been praised for their "rapt and fathomless spiritual intensity" by *American Record Guide*, and the Gloriæ Dei Cantores Schola, which specializes in the study and performance of Gregorian chant. Paraclete is also the exclusive North American distributor of the recordings of the Monastic Choir of St. Peter's Abbey in Solesmes, France, long considered to be a leading authority on Gregorian chant performance.

Learn more about us at our Web site:
www.paracletepress.com, or call us toll-free at 1-800-451-5006.

808.0662
G8514

133180

You May Also Enjoy. . .

The Emmaus Readers
Listening for God in Contemporary Fiction
Edited by Susan M. Felch and Gary D. Schmidt

ISBN: 978-1-55725-543-3
228 pages, $17.95, Paperback

Stories matter. Sometimes it's a story that can best tell the truth.

When an eclectic group of nine friends—fiction-readers and professors at Calvin College in Michigan—came together weekly to wrestle with great contemporary novels, they were surprised to discover how much spiritual meat they found. Together, the self-described Emmaus Readers read P.D. James, Ron Hansen, Ian McEwan, Yann Martel, Oscar Hijuelos, Frederick Buechner, and several others, across a variety of genres: historical fiction, fantasy, graphic novels, science fiction, and mystery.

Fiction from Paraclete Press

This Heavy Silence
Nicole Mazzarella

ISBN: 978-1-55725-508-2
250 pages, $14.95, Paperback

Winner
2006 Christy Award
Winner, Christianity Today
Book Award

When Dottie adopts her best friend's daughter out of a combination of spite and loyalty, she must confront her own ideas on motherhood, loneliness, love, and God.

Saving Erasmus
Steven Cleaver

ISBN: 978-1-55725-498-6
220 pages, $21.95, Hardcover

Named one of the
"Top Ten Christian Novels of 2007"
by both ALA Booklist *and*
Publishers Weekly

"Readers looking for something fresh and a little different from the usual heavyhanded fare in spiritual fiction will enjoy this slim novel. Highly recommended."
—*Library Journal*, starred review

Available from most booksellers or through Paraclete Press
www.paracletepress.com; 1-800-451-5006
Try your local bookstore first.

3 4711 00230 5862